NAVIGATING THROUGH CORPORATE WORLD

- Some Challenges

Impact of Company Culture on Performance & Results

HARCHARAN SINGH

Copyright © Harcharan Singh 2025
All Rights Reserved.

ISBN
Paperback 979-8-89673-711-7
Hardcase 979-8-89724-280-1

This book has been published with all efforts taken to make the material error-free after the consent of the author. However, the author and the publisher do not assume and hereby disclaim any liability to any party for any loss, damage, or disruption caused by errors or omissions, whether such errors or omissions result from negligence, accident, or any other cause.

While every effort has been made to avoid any mistake or omission, this publication is being sold on the condition and understanding that neither the author nor the publishers or printers would be liable in any manner to any person by reason of any mistake or omission in this publication or for any action taken or omitted to be taken or advice rendered or accepted on the basis of this work. For any defect in printing or binding the publishers will be liable only to replace the defective copy by another copy of this work then available.

Book

is

Dedicated

to

My Ancestors

Who dreamt & inspired

That

I will build my own future

Contents

Foreword

Mr. Harcharan Singh is quiet essentially a Maintenance Engineer who has to his credit a 5 decades of experience in big and small enterprises. A graduate in Mechanical engineering and Post graduate Diploma in Mechanical, Electrical and Metallurgy, he has worked in large and small enterprises for 5 decades in which he up graded the skill of workers and set up system which resulted in improved quality and productivity. He has mentored a large number of engineers and helped them to achieve their potential. He is sought after consultant by many enterprises to help them train their mangers and work men.

His book on his Journey emphasise on leadership, innovation and out of Box thinking to find solution to complex problem. This book will act as useful guide to all young engineers who are starting their career and have ambition to make mark.

I wish this attempt a great success and commend the effort of Mr. Harcharan Singh in writing this book which will help many in growth of their career.

J. Mehra
Former Chairman, RINL (Vizag Steel)
Vice Chairman (Metals & Minerals) Essar

Forword by B R Taneja ,
Ex- Managing Director, ISMT Limited
And Author of Book - The Making of ISMT

It is my pleasure to write a Forward for *Book- Navigating through Corporate World - Some Challenges & Impact of Company Culture on Performance & Result*s by Harcharan Singh and to introduce Mr. Harcharan Singh, Author of this book, who has more than 50 years of experience in plant engineering and operations roles, long back. We had appointed him as General Manager (Engineering) for our Indian Seamless Steels and Alloys Ltd., Pune, a Mini Alloys Steel plant in Jejuri, Pune. The newly setup plant had numerous teething problems and he played a Key Role in resolving them

He took leading role in setting up Working Systems in the Company. As Management Representative, he organized & coordinated to get Certifications of ISO9001, QS16949 Quality Management Systems, which were being sought urgently by Customers at that time. He organized Pollution Control Management ant Certifications for Plant very efficiently. He also took initiative to set up a Technical Training Centre at Plant site. He guided sister Company also in tackling technical plant problems and Pollution Control Projects & QS16949.

One of his specialties was that he always shouldered responsibility and held himself accountable for the function that he was heading and acted as a perfect shield for his subordinates to perform and blossom under his able leadership. In my interactions with me from the time, I have known him as a very soft spoken, humble technocrat who used to believe in teamwork

His book is about corporate culture and performance. As an organization evolves, its culture and capabilities evolve with it. Some of the key factors that impact corporate culture, sharing stories of companies who succeeded in transforming themselves — and those who failed. From small, family-run businesses to giant conglomerates, certain principles apply across the board.

He has touched few key questions: How do you influence positive change in mind-sets and behaviors across an organization?

Companies live and die by their culture. We'll look at the impact of training programs, work rituals, incentives structures and leadership.

What does it take to turn an underperforming asset into a high- performing one. How can companies generate more value from what they already have? How do some small companies build empires, while others stagnate.

Mr. Harcharan Singh has shared his personal experiences and thoughts in the form of this book and realized his much-cherished dream of his authoring his own book.

I am sure, the industry fraternity and Corporate world would be benefitted by his practical sharing of his thoughts and experiences.

I hope that all the readers will see most of achieving great milestones and learning and practicing by lessons given in this book.

Wishing him all the best,

Regards

B R Taneja
Ex-Managing Director, ISMT Limited
and Author of Book - The Making of ISMT

What Mr. R C NATHAN,
Owner, Nathan & Nathan Consultants Pvt Ltd,
Bengaluru has to say:

It is rightly said that People with a strong Shop Floor orientation are the best suited to offer realistic and practical guidance on manufacturing. The same can be extended to Corporate World. Such people need not be introduced. Their words and advice will speak for them. The above words sum up my understanding of Harcharan Singh.

You walk around any shop floor in India and you will see opportunities for learning, improvement, innovation and un-learning. There is no necessity to always try and bring something unique. Application of fundamentals and a sense of ownership is all that is needed to bring mammoth changes. This sums up my learning from Harcharan Singh.

I have known Harcharan Singh from his Tata Steel days but more closely when he was in ISMT Pune and his sincere work in the field of Scientific Maintenance has been using the principles of Total Productive Maintenance, Human Relations, Project Management, Excellent Communication and application of technology. When he presented to me the manuscript of his book, "Navigating through Corporate World – Some Challenges" the first think that struck me was the conversational style of writing. His vast experience is reflected in the title of each chapter which will attract anyone to read the chapter without putting the book down. He has kept the reader in mind while writing and not just his knowledge and experience. To me, these are profound down to earth way of communicating.

I had no hesitation in accepting to write this piece. There are several qualities of the author which you will see while reading this book.

The first one is versatility and completeness. I looked at the contents and it practically covers all aspects of a Corporate experience. One cannot come up with all these points unless one has been sufficiently grounded in the way Corporate functions

The next quality of the author is the manner in which the book is written. The chapters are written in a narrative which is like as though the author is talking to you. It is embedded with examples and stories which are easy to understand. I can confidently say that all kinds of corporate professionals will feel that their experience is captured well throughout out the book

This book is one example of customer focus – the key principle for success. In this context it is the Reader Focus. There are different types of readers. One is a serious reader who believes in systematically starting from the first page and going through in the same sequence as the book is written. Some are voracious and fast readers and would go quickly and look for priority areas to concentrate. Some are not habitual readers and generally look for something to catch their eye when reading so they continue to read. The author has written this book for any kind of reader. In fact, the first few sentences in each chapter will hook a reader in that chapter. Then there is brevity. It is not more than 3 to 4 pages and one can get a full view of the concept quickly. Next is the narrative which is like story telling. All put together it is both fun and useful reading.

The next quality of the author is the "Implementation" aspect. Harcharan Singh is a strong believer on actions. It is best understood throughout this book. The beauty is that it covers all conceivable aspects for effective implementation for a good professional executive in a company

We can go on with more such qualities of the author. But I don't want to stand in the reader's path to start reading the book. I am sure that every reader will benefit as per their objectives.

On a final note, please don't read the book without defining your objectives. Once you have defined your objectives and also your strengths and challenges, you will find that this book will come alive specifically for you. Such is the experience of authors like Harcharan Singh. My best wishes to all the readers in their managerial journey and someday hope to see most of you achieving great milestones.

Thank you

R C NATHAN

Owner

Nathan & Nathan Consultants Pvt Ltd, Bengaluru,

&

Author of Book

"I Can Make It Happen" – A Guide for actions

Acknowledgement

My acknowledgement for my first book –

First "I have to start by thanking my Wife & Children for encouraging me to pen down my life time experience. From reading early drafts to giving me advice on the cover. She was as important to this book getting done as I was. Thank you so much, dear Pammi." I would also like to thank her for me to not giving up on our dream of writing a book.

I'd also like to thank the many people who have helped me learn and practice both the Theory & Practices of Plant Engineering & maintenance throughout the years.

An additional thanks to my dear friends who read through the draft and provided meaningful feedback. I owe an enormous debt of gratitude to those who gave me detailed and constructive comments on one or more chapters.

They spared their time freely to discuss nuances of the text and pushed me to clarify concepts, explore particular facets of insight work, and explain the rationales for specific recommendations.

Preface

I realize that this book will be of interest to all connected with Corporate World. It has never been easy to challenge the consensus because the System – of any kind, in any context – will try to preserve the *status quo,* by all means possible.

Having spent over five decades in the field of Shop-floor activities management with great circle of Colleagues and friends, I feel obliged to share my knowledge and, analyses, and conclusions.

This book does not have only my story but of also of few friends, who shared their experience with me for the benefits of Readers of this book.

Hopefully, these accounts will raise the level of awareness among the general Corporate Employees and initiate the discussion that, in turn, may entail major cultural changes, as well as a revision of the approach to Corporate thinking towards its Operations.

To Readers, in Industry, few of the descriptions may sound familiar and they may tend to relate it to them. I apologies to them. Desecrations & Narrations are purely with the purpose of Readers to learn from the Incidences. It is not to hurt any ones' sentiments.

This book can be read on two different levels.

First, it may be read by ordinary people with Industry background. Throughout, the book has been written with this audience in mind. One of the important features of this book is that it does not have a textbook structure when the chapters, in order to be understood, need not be read in the sequence given. In fact, you can start the reading journey from any chapter, based on your interests, tastes, and preferences.

The second group of readers can people in management operating the companies and will be represented by professionals from the Manufacturing industry, & academia. I do not expect everybody to agree with the content and ideas put forth in this book. But I do hope that the information and knowledge presented will become a wake-up call for the general Industry Professionals.

I hope this book is widely read. If we are to avoid the blunders of the past, then we need to change the direction and start benefiting from the knowledge based on Systems in place & practical learning at work place. Although we did not have this chance few decades ago but now is the right time.

Chapter 1

Agent of Management – Navigating the Winds of Corporate Change

---

Change is the only constant in the world of business. New technologies, market disruptions, economic fluctuations - the corporate landscape is always shifting and evolving. This rapid change can be disorienting for even the most seasoned professionals. How do you stay agile and adapt successfully? How do you drive positive change at your own company?

Drawing from over 50 years of experience in plant engineering and operations roles, I've seen first hand and how change unfolds in corporations, for better or worse. In this book, I want to share the lessons I've learned to help you navigate the winds of change more skilfully.

At its core, this book is about corporate culture and performance. As an organization evolves, its culture and capabilities evolve with it. I will distill some of the key factors that impact corporate culture, sharing stories of companies who succeeded in transforming themselves - and those who failed. From small, family-run businesses to giant conglomerates, certain principles apply across the board.

Here are some of the key questions we'll explore together:

- How do you influence positive change in mind-sets and behaviours across an organization? Companies live and die by their culture. We'll look at the impact of training programs, work rituals, incentives structures and leadership.

- What does it take to turn an underperforming asset into a high-performing one? Mentorship, opportunities, and flexibility are key.

- How can companies generate more value from what they already have? There are endless ways to utilize resources more efficiently, from assets to raw materials to people's time and skills.

- How do you balance delivering short-term results with long-term investments? Managing budgets, inventory and strategic trade-offs is an art and science.

- Why do some companies bounce back from crises while others crumble? From quality control failures to plant accidents, we'll look at contributing factors.

- How does the quality of management impact employees' performance and morale? From lighting fires to leading by example, management style matters.

- What separates successful international expansions from disappointing ones? On-the-ground realities can make or break overseas ventures.

- How do some small companies build empires, while others stagnate? Hints: Flexibility, family involvement, and embracing partnerships.

These are complex, multifaceted areas with no easy answers. There is no master formula I can prescribe. However, I hope by transparently sharing experiences - mine and others' - we can have an insightful dialogue and think more critically about these issues.

The corporate world needs more open, honest examinations of what works, what doesn't, and why. My goal is not to criticize but to expand awareness of different growth paths. I invite you to learn alongside me. With knowledge and courage, we can create more conscious, successful, and sustainable business cultures together.

Let's begin the journey.

AGENT OF MANAGEMENT:

Two decades earlier, one of the Plant of Reputed fine quality papers making Company, assigned me for conducting *Work ethics & Work Culture* workshop for their workers. It used to be two days training programme to cover all the workers below 55 years age, retirement age being 58 years. I conducted programmes for over 20 batches.

The programme was initiated with the purpose to uplift morale of workers, as many of aging workers had been given VRS-Voluntary Retirement, while rationalising manpower. But, Employees were not ready to accept and were feeling demoralised.

For every batch, Normally, Initial reaction of participants on the first day used to be that I was an Agent of Management sent to brain wash them. But in every Training batch, at half day of lunch break while discussing between themselves, they found that lessons were meaningful to them and their work & family life. So they started getting interested for listening to me from second half.

One of the clever worker even tried to bring on hostility in the group by asking provocating questions, one of them was that management has been giving differential treatment, giving example that I (the faculty) was being provided sealed Bisleri Water Bottle, while all workers in the class room were given water from their Aqua Guard in regular unsealed bottles. I could see hostility in the group of Senior Workers in the hall. I did not know how to satisfy the group, so I took a chance of asking him a question,

"What was his son doing? to which he proudly answered that his son was a Software Engineer in Bangalore and getting salary double than him. So I could confront him by making my observation that if his son's gets recognition by his employers, it is perfectly okay with you. When your company does the same with the learned Faculty, travelling from distance, then you consider it unfair. I said let us hear your Co-Workers to which all the participants in the hall, gave their warm approval Nods. With this the atmosphere in the room changed for better.

I explained them how important was this employment for them with very good salary, which they started to accept. On the second day end, at the Valedictory function review by the plant head, the hall was full and all the participants gave a good feedback. Even before that one of the senior officer on the dais asked me how was the programme, to which his HRD Head sitting next to us did not wait for my answer, and commented that had the programme been less interesting you will find hall half empty, as the workers there do not hesitate to leave room, even in MD's meeting, if they do not find it to their meaning & interesting enough.

Later two participants visited me in Guest House and appreciated the lessons which I had shared with them and confessed that this workshop has changed their mind-set to develop a Positive Attitude towards life, While taking leave, they both bowed & touched my feet to get blessings. I shared this incidence with my wife, who was always feeling that I was terror in my plant, so employees visiting me at my home sometime from plant, some time had bowed & touched my feet. I explained to her that my Subordinates respected me, because they valued the guidance, coaching & support, which they received from me.

– *Moral* –

For Employees' Attitude & Skill upgradation, appropriate Training is worth investing.

Chapter 2

Making of Zero to Hero

I am sharing experience of one of my friend, Prashant. In his midcareer, one of my friend was given a job offer & invited to join a Company to centralize Maintenance and Engineering Activities of a cold rolling, Galvanizing and Colour coating line plant. As head of Engineering, he had to bring all maintenance, engineering activities, workshop, boilers etc in a centralized department.

Immediately on joining, among other documents, his office Assistant handed him dismissal letter of three Dy. Managers, to be handed over to concerned. He felt that it would very demoralizing to make his entry to the department with such an unpleasant task, so he checked up with the President, plant head, what to do and he allowed to decide whatever he wanted to do about it.

He talked to all three and they already knew about it and ready to leave town with their luggage packed and children's admissions arranged already in other towns.

He offered them one Chance and two of them opened up. Basic reason was both did not toe Management unreasonable approaches and unrealistic deadlines. One was mechanical and out blunt & frank and second one was Electronics Engineer.

Both were dedicated passionate Maintenance Engineers (Degree Holders).

Both knew the Top Management directly, personally & closely and made effort to make me understand that Top person had already made up his mind and their office staff had informed them & asked them to pack off. As he (HOD) persisted, they agreed try out an experiment.

For next few months, he personally on daily monitored & supervised their activities with direct control. They took up massive Modification activities making huge cost saving and productivity improvement. In every weekly meeting of plant chaired by President, improvement activities done in areas of these Dy. Managers were recorded in MOM (minutes of meeting) which was sent to corporate office. Some times there were side talks that these improvement jobs have been done by HOD himself. But no one dared to speak out.

Then came then Annual Appraisal time and he recommended them to promoted both to manager post, already due, which was agreed by the Sr. Vice President and both became Managers. In case of Electronics person, he had been previously been fitted in much lower salary slab at the time of his appointment as he was very shy & simple person.

My friend made a strong case of Anomaly in salary Slab and recommended a good raise to bring it in par with his Colleagues. This was also accepted by the Management. So they had two satisfied sectional heads making good contribution. Electronics person got chance of going abroad for selection of New Equipment.

M.D used to make one / two visits to the plant every year. During one of visit in lunch Hosted by him to senior officers, he asked my friend, Prashant what special he was doing?

Prashant replied that few projects are under implementation but most satisfying out of them one was to make –"Hero of people declared zero" by the Management.

He graciously agreed and acknowledged his leadership ability. After some time after few years of work, Prashant moved to other organization. But both of these person got further raises up to General Managers in their respective area, that is what my friend heard later on.

– *Moral* –

Leadership matters.

Person leaves but his Foot Prints remain.

Chapter 3

"Black Patches – Darkening Careers"

Our cold Steel Rolling Mill was making & supplying steel sheets for auto cars & bus body panel parts as well as white good appliances like fridge & washing machines. Suddenly there were heavy rejections of material due to black patches appearing on cold rolled steel sheets. Dispatches were kept on hold to find the cause and to remove the defects.

Quality Department reported the cause to be rolling Mill Roll Cooling Coolants carryover of coolant emulsion staining the sheets. Air-whipping Nozzles are provided on the outlets of the Mill to wipe out the coolant coming out with the rolled strip.

We changed the coolant and also repeatedly attended to Air Nozzles, ensuring they worked effectively. But Black Patches continued causing heavy losses to the company.

Operation Head and Quality Dept. head both teamed together to put all the blame on the Maintenance Dept. we could not defend ourselves, meanwhile annual appraisals were carried out in this atmosphere, all the concerned Maintenance staff including Engineering Head suffered and missed promotion due.

Management also continued to get testing done by other outside independent laboratories. It was later on discovered that specification of HR (Hot Rolled) Steel Coils Imported from South Korea did not meet the application requirements. Earlier HR Coils were obtained from RSP Rourkela, who were using same material in their own Rolling also and material specification was perfect and no Black Patches problem was ever faced. As raw material inventory in our Plant was stored together for both RSP and South Korea H.R. Coils. When RSP Coils were rolled, there was no black patches problem and as major stock was imported HR Coils, black patches problem would restart.

H.R. Coils had been imported from South Korea as they gave Price discount, making their coils cheaper. Our management being mainly business family tried to save cost as much as and wherever it was possible. Later on, specifications were fine-tuned and black patches problem, disappeared, as it was never due to lapse on the part of mill maintenance.

– *Moral* –

Only hard Work is not enough, not even Smart work.

Some time, Luck and situation have its own Role. Some time, there are Bad Coincidences.

Chapter 4

"Maintenance Budget and Spare Parts Inventory"

When I took charge of Engineering and Maintenance Department in new plant, I found that spares requisition was raised only after the breakdown.

This caused delay in repair and longer downtime. On checking, I was told that Maintenance Budget is very tight and staff have to work within the budget. Hence Department was unable to maintain stock of essential spares. On checking with management, their observation was maintenance spares were major part of Plant store inventory.

To ease the situation immediate actions were initiated as described below. Consumption share as per Computer statement printed with following groups of maintenance items was as given below:

I.   Non-Moving items =50%

II. Spares drawn with period more than three years- Slow moving items =20%

III. Regular consumption=30%

Experienced staff team was formed to scrutinise the list and finding was that more 40% items were not needed by the department, as spares were either obsolete or non-useable.

These were offered for disposal suitably. Hence, store inventory drastically reduced.

During my plant round, I found that many repairable Machine assemblies lying in Departmental yards. We arranged for its recondition and to keep these in the main store for future use. These were tested & tagged and signed by authorized Engineer that these were useable.

These were stocked at zero cost in Store but management agreed us to give 50% credit of its cost/price. This credit was added to departmental budget and gave us opportunity to increase the spare withdrawal budget limit. So, purchase of essential spares became possible and helped to control breakdown repair time.

"Standardization":

Components & Assemblies of various brands like Siemens, Kirloskar, IBM, Crompton's are used in Electrical Equipment procured by plants and hence it becomes necessary to keep inventory stock of all the brands for replacement items in case the component failure. Effort was made to reduce brands and decide on one / two makes for future equipment purchases. For new purchases, equipment manufacturers & suppliers were asked to use brands selected by us. This helped to ensure that replacement components and assemblies could be maintained in stock in store. This also helped to reduce inventory in store.

VARIETY REDCUTION:

As there were too many sizes & varieties of components in use, a plant survey was done to find out the detailed data. For example, V-Belts of A-40, A-42, A-44 and hydraulic hoses-18" long, 20", 22" & 24" were used on machines supplied by different OEM's (Original Equipment Suppliers) and spare of each size were stocked in store, thus increasing store inventory.

It was possible to reduce the number of sizes of these components with or without making minor modifications. Rubber items have limited shelf-life, which means that these items cannot be stored for more than 2/3 years, Even if not taken by consuming department, these have to be scrapped & sent for disposal after its shelf life is reached. This point is also verified in every 1SO-9001 audits. This variety reduction exercise helped in reducing store inventory.

– Moral –

For establishing a high standard System in the Plant, Management need to hire Competent HODs with solid good technical experience background.

Chapter 5

My Career Start – First 28 Days and Thereafter

In my first job, I joined as Graduate Trainees in an Integrated Steel Plant, after Engineering Degree, and on completing one and half year of training, which is considered to be world class standard, we were assigned our department. I was able to select Power Engineering, prestigious department and was placed in their Steam Turbine Overhauling Section. It had around 35 Technicians and used to go to different locations as per Turbine and Turbo blowers Repair & overhaul schedule.

At that point of time, it was being headed by an acting foreman. We had American plant designations like Chargeman, Foreman, Asst. General foreman, Master Mechanic & Master roll turner, First hand and Second hand. The Girls from native Villages getting married to second hands had tough time explaining to their relatives that second hand is one of post in steel melting shops.

As our section had full standard force manpower, I was added as extra to standard force and not eligible for Incentive Bonus, which was about 40-45% of Total Salary at that time. My technical capability and interpersonal skills were being monitored and after only 28 days, I was formally installed as foreman & given charge of section and earlier acting foreman started reporting to me being the chargeman in the section.

There were many challenges waiting. We had two long beard Sikh Sardarji as Super craftsmen, post retirement. They used to do re-blading of steam turbine rotors, as they had earlier worked long time with foreign experts and after getting trained them, who had been called to repair & replace damaged blades of the turbines. Super craftsman is as special designation, outside regular grades of company. This does not any fixed grade and there is No retirement age for them.

As our super boss asst. HOD also had been himself had worked as trainee with them in his initial days, so he was very close to them and they freely discussed departmental affairs.

Although I was sectional Incharge but none of senior technician was giving due respect or wishing me when we met in the morning. Once I raised these point with them and their comment was that I had earn it first by being technically competent. On being challenged, they suggested a competition with them in finishing Babbit Metal Mitchel thrust pads, by scrapping it. As I had undergone practical skill training of filing, fitting & chipping during my training, I managed to make it sufficiently well to their standard. so I passed the Test and pads were used by them for replacement of damaged ones.

Then I did think of building some pressure to have more control on them to get better output. Once, We had case of Turbine bearing cooling oil leakage on turbo-blower and a bucket was kept by them to collect leakage oil, which was hated by our Seniors' as it indicated sub - standard maintenance. I asked them to tighten the pipe- joint to stop leakage but they wanted a shutdown, but getting Equipment shutdown was difficult procedure and required proper justification. As this was not attended in spite of my reminders, I myself went up the hot location and tightened hot oil 50/55° c temp joint of the pipe and oil leakage stopped. Although I had blisters on hands but I posed hero and was accepted as their leader. Thereafter, I could walk with my head high with authority.

Next step was develop efficiency and ease of work. As the Power Plant was quite old and pipeline fitting of steam as well as water line required frequent replacement. To draw these items from store, a material requisition was required and to make it separately for every item with its stock item required lot time to be spent, as technicians gave a long list of small items every week. I identified one literate helper, who was interested in paper work and trained him do it this non-productive job. He too was happy that he did not have to do dirty work. Thereafter, I just had sign and scrutinise that he did not make a mistake.

Later in career, when lot of correspondence needed to done, correct spelling was always a challenge. This was solved by just chance. I found that our tea boy was a graduate, so I took an English dictionary from home and he used to check & correct spelling mistakes in all my draft, thus saving time.

– *Moral* –

Well Planned & implemented Corporate Training Programme for fresh Trainees can and does prepare young Engineers take up senior positions, even to lead the Company up to MD position in future.

Chapter 6

One German Equal to Seven Indians

In our mini steel plant, we had a German Engineer, deputed by Demag German company, to compile operational data of one of few three rolls planetary steel rolling mills in the World. He was lonely soul working stand alone in our country side plant, During my morning shop floor round, as being Engineering Head, I used to spend sometime as courtesy call & take coffee also sometime. In course of discussions, he always used to share his observation on productivity level of our workers, with a comment quite frequently that "seven Indian workers equal to one German worker", making me uncomfortable. But I never challenged because I too regard German Workers in high esteem.

Once we had a major breakdown on this rolling mill and it became necessary to cut 2.5"inches dia. stainless steel bolt nuts. As gas cutting was not permitted on this equipment, our fitters' team was struggling to cut stainless nut for whole morning but were unable to make much progress. We had limited period shutdown and likely to once again fail to complete the job in scheduled period.

Suddenly, I remembered his repeated made comments. Although as Engineer, he had been working on laptop only for last full year, still I thought of making fun of him. On my request, he did not hesitate for a moment. He picked up a 10 kg hammer instead of 5 kg used by our fitters and chiselled out the nut in two piece in about 45 minutes, non-stop. The whole management team & staff present there were stunned. After completing the job, he went back to his office, triumphed, though he might have got severe blisters in his soft hands. That was a lesson to all us, though this was never discussed any were.

This tells us, how practical plant training is important to build up skill competence. Practical training to employees for the skill development is important factor for improving their productivity. Few reputed companies like Tata steel & Tata motors and many others have huge training Institutes with facilities for practical hands-on training for employees.

Few companies provide even engineering courses which are recognized by the company equivalent to degree in Engineering. Tata steel has such eight year course.

Even, Few of fitters have been able to rise to level of department HOD through these courses & self-learning programmes. One Superintendent of Wheel Tyre & Axle plant of Tata steel was one such example. Jindal & Bajaj Auto and few others have also built up good employees Training centres. Few other companies too had taken initiative to establish expensive training excellence centres but could not sustain its maintenance and these were closed down.

– Moral –

Practical on the Job Training for Employees & Efficiency Tests help in keeping Staff Productive.

Chapter 7

Safety First Approach to LPG Pipeline – Modification for 80 ton LPG-BULLET

In our steel cold rolling & galvanizing plant, LPG Gas is used for heating & annealing furnaces. LPG Gas is stored in a 80 Tonnes bullets (gas storage tanks; called as bullets) and LPG pipe line -18" diameter ring main goes around the whole Building shed.

In our plant, as a result of various capacity enhancing projects, production had increased.

For this, for increasing length of cold rolling mill shed, few more columns needed adding. This required removing the existing LPG pipeline by cutting and re-routing. We had placed work order on a reputed LPG contractor Expert and obtained management approval for two days shutdown of total plant from corporate Kolkata Head office. At Last moment, LPG expert had some family tragedy & contractor failed to come for the job. As LPG pipeline cutting job was very risky with bullets full of highly explosive LPG, a small lapse can cause total explosion of the plant.

As head of Engineering, I was personally co-ordinator of executing this shutdown and to reschedule to a later date, meant that total shed extension project work would be delayed. We had working team meeting to understand detail activities required. Though no one had undertaken such job but our staff had always been associated, since long time with the LPG contractor & experts.

Finally, we decided not to postpone & to take up the activity. So I had to lead the group by my personal presence all the time which meant standing on the shop floor for 18 hours continuously and closely monitoring, analysing and co-ordinating all the safety steps.

That Job involved purging the full pipeline with nitrogen & testing that no trace of LPG gas is left in the pipeline. Cutting the existing pipe-line, connecting New ring main pipeline.

Top management had minute to minute updates and was very keenly & closely keeping the watch but never interfered. The pipeline job of re- routing was completed 4 hours ahead of schedule and line was charged with LPG Gas and plant was re-started.

I came home & almost fell in the bed for flat twelve hours rest. No-one never made any comment of difficult task well completed and was just considered normal shutdown activity.

– Moral –

– Plant Managers are constantly responsible for taking risky decisions for maintaining non- interrupted smooth operation and have to take calculated Risk-related decisions for going up in their Career and this affects their Health. This is professional hazard for high performing Managers.

Chapter 8

Gemba KAIZEN in Indian Mini Steel Plant in as Early as 1992

Implementing KAIZEN practices in Indian Mini Steel Plants in as early as in 1992 was rare. There were only few progressive Companies which had world wise connections and practicing Good Productivity Tools & Techniques. Our Company had Contract with a Japanese Trained Kaizen Expert Consultant to implement Kaizen Activities. He Trained Selected staff in the Company to understand the Methodology.

All Supervisors had to report every month Improvements made by him personally & his team. If he did an improvement himself, he would earn one point but he will get 2 points, if he implemented other's Idea. This encouraged people to Cooperate and do Team improvements. As head of Engineering, my area of control was full Plant, I was always at top in number of improvements made every Month.

Kaizen Expert's representative used to conduct Kaizen monthly Review meetings of small groups of different levels, where each one had report of improvement made by him and his team in 3 to 5 minutes. Even if one had nothing to report, Group members had to sit silently for 3 minutes. This would put mental pressure for him to do and report improvements in next month.

Kaizen is very low / no investment improvements method. Besides Kaizen, we were also doing major modifications.

When I took over as head of engineering of a cold rolling, galvanizing & colour coating line, plant has numerous problems but these were not being highlighted as capacity utilization of plant was around 50% , so all the defects were attended during the period when plant was not in operation. By the time, I joined, order booking for products had already improved and soon plant started operating on full Capacity and downtown figures also started rising, as there was no idle time. At that time compliance of Maintenance P.M. (Preventive Maintenance) checklist was also barely 70% , resulting in lot of backlogs. Explanation was, always manpower shortage.

After brain storming, we revised our P.M. Schedule by increasing period between P.M. Jobs, thus decreasing the number of P.M. lists to be done during the month and also planned to finish all scheduled P.M. checklist to be completed by 25th of month. Balance period was used to do any backlogs.

One other important factor, Pickling rolls drive D.C. motors were failing was very frequent and these burnt motors were regularly sent for rewinding. Pickling line shed used to be full of hydrochloric acid fumes, as hot acid bath was used to pickling / cleaning HR (hot rolled) steel strips by removing its rust.

As D.C. Motors carbon lugs & Commutaters were made of copper wires, these used to get oxidized and get damaged due to exposure to HCL Acid fumes. After brain storming, we installed a blower, outside the building, to supply fresh cooling air for the D.C. motors and problem was significantly reduced.

"QUANTUM IMPROVEMENT OF INCREASING CGL-STEEL SHEET GALVANISING LINE SPEED"

In our plant, maximum operating line speed of Continuous Galvanising Line - CGL had 90 metres/minutes and average operating speed was 60m/min. Uncoiler motor was rated to run at 130 meters/min & so was recoiler motor but all the other drives had 90 meters/min speed limit. We had discussion of increasing the line speed but understanding of shop-floor staff was that it would become expensive project, so even top management could never demand but they were very keen to increase CGL production as the order books were overbooked and the demand has increased.

I kept having brainstorming with different shop floor engineers and found a way out. We found a way to do it without major investment. Speed of D.C Motors of non-Ox soaking furnace driving roller could be increased by its field weakening. Speed of mechanical drive chains drive could be increased by replacing driving sprockets by smaller diameters to get reduced speed reduction ratio. So solution ended up to easy and practical actions.

By making these modifications, over a period of three months, we could achieve maximum line speed of 130 meters/min and average speed of line to 90 meters/min. This resulted in capacity of CGL line production increase by 50% for free.

It was also required to use bigger size C.R. (cold roller) coils of 12T to meet feeding rate instead of 9T used earlier.

As the EOT crane capacity was only 10 tonnes, EOT crane was also modified by reputed Competent Certified crane contractor, who strengthened the crane girders & also gantry columns and capacity was increased to 12T and got crane load tested and certificate to use crane at higher rating.

– Moral –

Opportunities for making improvements in any operation are many. There is so much inefficiency in our operating Systems, there no end to limit for making Improvements.

Chapter 9

Dealing with Manufacturing Defects, after Warranty Period

Some Case Studies
1.   Coopers' vertical boring machine.
2.   Mukund's Heavy Duty EOT cranes.
3.   Kirloskar pneumatic reciprocating Air compressors.
4.   Siemens PLC Electronic Cards.

No manufacturer wants their Equipment to underperform and downgraded, blacklisted or likes to get their brand name & reputation to go down. I will just narrate three cases of three different companies.

First one happened in Jamshedpur in 1988. We had failure of a big roller bearing on Cooper's vertical boring machine. On dismantling the machine it was discovered that although a lubricating point for bearing was provided outside but they missed cut a groove at the bearing for the lubricant to enter. The machine has been purchased few years earlier but was never used much. After the initial fill of bearing got consumed, the bearing failed. Even at time in 1988, cost of this Bearing would be few lakhs.

The company was informed of the failure and their technical representative visited to inspect & investigate the failure. While going through my round, I too, said hello to him and made a passing comment. "Coopers are known for their quality" and their Management would be shocked to learn about such a lapse of a manufacturing defect. As the machine is not under warranty period, we cannot make the claim o replace the bearing.

Later purchase department informed me that visitor was himself directors of the company and he readily accepted lapse on their part and he immediately had ordered free replacement bearing to be dispatched. But Purchase department took the credit from management of handling the case so well.

Second Case one is for 150T hot metal EOT cranes supplied and erected by Mukand's contractor team. One of the hoist shaft ball bearing failed after five years in operation and investigation report of Mukund concluded that its happened due to jerky operation of the crane and not original equipment defect. In my inspection during failure investigation, I had seen shining marks on the broken bearing races, which cannot happen due to sudden breakage. My logic was that bearing was not properly fitted and balls of the bearing had been rubbing for long period, causing silvery shine on the races. I took the failed bearing and discussed with their head of crane design but he avoided the issue. But their vice president intervened and at very look of bearing, he commented that it is a erection lapse and possible that this bearing on other cranes may also fail. He ordered new bearings with proper precaution to be fitted by Mukund Contractor on all the eight cranes- bearings and labour all free. Which was done over next few months. Problem never reoccurred.

Third Case - Next case is of reciprocating air compressor- 26 m^3/ min. capacity with overhang drive pulley. The overhang belt drive pulley shaft broke in two pieces. We made a good case about its design and got free replacement of new air compressor from Kirloskar Pneumatics Company. Overhang belt drive pulley shaft and compressor shaft are coupled with solid coupling as the whole assembly of two shafts is supported by only three bearings. Solid coupling alignment requires both shaft to become co-axial after alignment. This is very difficult task for shop floor technicians. A good case was made and better design equipment was received as free replacement. This is worked trouble free for long period.

Next one is of Siemens PLC cards in 1993.

Although ours was very modern mini Steel Rolling Mill with high level of automation in 1993, But this too had its own challenges. All the lines of cold steel rolling mill, CGL – Galvanising line & coating line were all Siemens PLC controlled.

Mainly two challenges were
I.   PLC going into stop mode in Pickling line
II. After P.M preventive maintenance of electronic equipment, malfunctioning of the line,

Although I am mechanical engineer but had to spend more time in finding system solutions for electronic equipment. First action which we took was to keep only electronic engineer in shift duty and brought electrical engineers working in shifts to general shift, as electrical engineers were unable to rectify PLC problems.

Second problem of line malfunctioning was tackled by putting ban on disconnecting connectors of electronic equipment at time of preventive maintenance. As these cable contactors have many pin & knobs and if any one did not fit properly, it would result in loose connection. So Only air blowing & vacuum cleaning was allowed to be done during the maintenance. These steps greatly reduced frequent breakdowns of electrical / electronics equipment and malfunctioning of the lines. Implementing the above steps were not easy, as it caused lot of shop-floor discipline related actions.

But the PLC of H.R. (hot rolled) steel coil sheets in pickling line going into stop mode problem could not be solved. We had many fine electronics Engineers but no one had any suggestion what to do! Finally, I decide to visit Siemens H.O. in Mumbai as their service engineers, who were frequently called to attend the Siemens PLC system but had given no permanent solution.

In Siemens office, their G.M. listened to us and I still remembered his remarks that "Siemens is a sleeping giant". Now that I had knocked their door, problem would be resolved. He took us to their vice-president, who immediately arranged our meeting with their quality team, who asked our electronics engineer to give them all the technical details and they also kept two failed PLC cards which had taken with us, I think pickling line roll drives had more than twenty such PLC card.

Their service engineer visited after about two week, with repaired cards, after fitting these, he took more defective cards with him for repair.

We were hold that some switch has problem which was modified / replaced and all the old card were taken to their repair centre and repaired. This whole exercise by Siemens was free of any cost. We appreciate their professional approach. The PLC stop mode problem in pickling line became thing of past.

– *Moral* –

All reputed Suppliers are Quality conscious and they take care of their Brand Name by meeting & exceeding Customers' expectations. Customer & Supplier relationship is important.

Reminded me of an old Case of Merced Benz Car –

In olden time, Maharaja of Baroda had few Mercedes Benz Cars. And Axle of one Car broke, you know the Condition of Indian Roads in olden times and even at places. So telegram was sent to Germany, Technicians with Axle was brought by Flight and Car was urgently repaired.

While checking on Bills, *Company said no bills, because Mercedes Benz Cars axles don't break.*

Chapter 10

Stealing of Company Property & Wastage Control – How Stopped

In continuous casting mini steel plants, hot blooms are cut with oxy-gas torches by auto cutters, where pieces can be cut to pre determined length by Auto cutters, controlled through computerized automation systems.

It was found that oxygen gas consumption per tonne of hot steel blooms was very high. But, no solution could be found, as oxy gas cutters to work effective, high O2 gas cylinder pressure is required.

On monitoring & measuring O2 gas cylinders pressures for the incoming full lot, we discovered that few of re-filled gas cylinders received from gas company were empty. Some of Empty cylinders returned to Gas company also were found to be full. So later on, during surprise checks, we found that in full truck received with full refilled cylinders, few empty cylinders were being received. Empty cylinders being returned were not getting fully empty for Technical reasons. Pressure of refilled full cylinders varied from 115 to 125 psi (lbs/square inch) instead of standard specification of above 140 psi.

These checks and monitoring made all concerned alert and we started getting O2 gas pressure above 135psi in all the cylinders. Due to lower pressure at users end, cylinders even with liquid O2 with more than 5kg were being returned for refilling.

Concept of O2 cylinder bank containing 12 nos in one tray interconnected with each others assured higher pressure with less gas in them so better utilization.

For cooking, canteen used to take full new LPG cylinders from store. There also, we started giving them used cylinders from plant and made bank of cylinders so that even with cylinders which were partly full, could be used. This made it possible for them to get gas, partly free or at lower cost.

Mini Steel Plants buy Steel Scrap for Making various types of Alloy Steels. Steel Scrap is stored in separate yard where it segregated grade wise. Can you imagine that you find pile of Truck Tyres laying all over. Very few Senior officer go to scrap yard, unless there is dispute to be sorted out.

I have the habit of making regular round of the Plant, even Now any Factory, I visit, I make a long Round, you can find a lot about the Condition and Areas where improvement is required.

Coming to the point of Tyres in the Scrap yard, no one concerned could give any explanation. So, while taking Lunch, I pointed to Plant Head about the Tyres. He was very sharp. He said we are getting junk tyres in place of Steel. We discovered that old rejected Tyres & Tubes full of Water were brought to increase the Gross Weight and Tyres were removed from the truck & Tubes emptied to record more load of material. So immediately Action was taken to prevent further loss.

– *Moral* –

Management and Senior Officers need to vigilant all the time, otherwise there are people (Vultures) every where ready to rob Company property.

Chapter 11

Resources Management – Wastages Control & Energy Saving

Industrial Cooling Water Management: The plant in question had a big water Pond / reservoir for taking care of cooling water requirement of a Mini steel mill. Cooling Water was brought through a big pipeline from a lake. While making water balance sheet, it was found that about 20% water was getting lost through leaking/ soaking to underground, as its water proofing, which is provided at the bottom, while constructing the water reservoir tank, had failed. A long shutdown for its repair and budget for funds were not available at that time, After lot of Brainstorming, four bore wells were dug in its corners and leaked water was collected, which was directly pumped to daily water supply overhead tank to recover around 15% of total water. This greatly reduced the water consumption cost and pumping energy bill.

Further, few deep well submersible pumps were installed for watering big garden of the plant spread over many acres, thus helping to reduce the purchased water consumption. Deep Bore wells water having TDS (over 3000ppm Total dissolves solids) was unsuitable for plant cooling water application.

Oxygen Gas Cylinders: For reducing the consumption of oxygen gas, a system of making bank of cylinders helped in maintaining gas line pressure and reduce the consumption by improving its utilization.

Day Light Utilization: Fixing transport sheets on the shed roof helped to switch off light bulbs during the day. This also helped to save energy.

Compressed Air Management: Compressed air pipeline leakage test helped to locate and repair/stop leaks.

Air leakage was calculated to around 25 to 30% . This action helped to reduce air compressor energy bill. All the heat exchangers cooling tubes were cleaned by brush or by chemical cleaning. This improved performance of the heat exchangers and the equipment.

Canteen Food quality:

While visiting Canteen, found Vegetables & Grains stored on floor with Rats damaging the raw material. This was also effecting the quality of food prepared & served in canteen. Proper Storage racks were made for keeping Vegetables & grains. Sanitation level was improved. Employees could get Hygienic food.

Store & Master Specifications:

In Store, material was again overflowing because of shortage of space. Concept of Vertical Storage with Racks with Shelves was introduced. Heavy material was kept at ground / lower level and lighter material in higher selves. And Store Capacity increased to store much more material.

Mater Specifications were reviewed by experienced person of Maintenance Department. Lot discrepancies were corrected. This insured that Material with correct Specification was ordered.

Earlier many items had been rejected by our engineers doing incoming- material inspection for Store to send this material back to Vendor / Supplier for replacement or correction. I used to advise the Plant persons to re-check material with the description / specification given in Purchase order copy and with material received, as their Payment is made on satisfactory supply of material, Vendors would not normally make mistake. our Company would have to pay, if material was as per Purchase order. So the sectional Head making the material requisition will be answerable.

In many cases wrong or defective material had to be drawn by the department to avoid management questioning. Therefore, review of Master Specifications of store material is very necessary.

Healthiness of Relays and protections:
While doing Breakdown analysis of Equipment failing because Relays and protections being inoperative. We found that mostly primary protection, which was not functioning previously, had been bypassed to keep the equipment working on secondary protection.

A plant wise Survey was conducted which discovered that more twenty percent equipment were operating on second protection and susceptible to failing any time. Timely action could be taken to make equipment availability more reliable.

Suggestions & Recommendations for Cost saving:
Any company can reduce cost by measuring and monitoring Material & Consumables Consumption.

ABC analysis is done to find out items contributing to major expenditure. Major items could include - Lubricants

Consumption., Bearings, Electric motors, Pumps. With systematic study followed by suitable actions always results in great savings.

Improvements in sister Company:

Elsewhere in other sister company plant, where undersigned was invited to advice to implement such ideas.

It was reported by that plant staff that hydraulic oil-seals were leaking & failing due to high oil temperature. It was noted that recirculating cooling water was dirty and inlet water going to heat Exchangers itself had temp after cooling pond was up to 35*C.

It was observed that plant make- up water from MIDC at around 30* C temperature was being pumped into cooling pond which also had dirty & hot plant return water from plant.

Modification in the water pipeline was made for MIDC cool 30*C water to directly go for cooling critical systems, including hydraulic power packs, which was brought to makeup plant water supply. This straight away helped constant supply of Clean Water with 5*C cooler temperature. This greatly improved the performance of vital equipment.

– Lesson –

It is possible to do RESOURCES WASTAGES CONTROL & ENERGY SAVING.

What is required is Measuring and Monitoring Consumptions & Performance Parameters.

Chapter 12

Successful & Failed Overseas' Ventures

People, skilled, qualified and experienced, go abroad to make high income. Gulf countries are more profitable as the salaries are generally in par with West but no income tax is to be paid. Language is also more comfortable, as many Indians and Pakistanis are working in most of the technical plants. Gulf is paradise for trade skilled workers, where they can personally perform, like welders, Electrician and plumbers, and they make good earnings. They will not fail.

Challenges for senior managerial positions are different. Here in India, we have team of competent subordinate staff at every level and the HOD can manage only with his managerial & analytical skills and can get results to meet, even exceed, management expectations and targets. So here, dedicated professionals will not fail, unless they become victim of corporate politics, If the person is smart and tactful, he can perform well even up to two levels up.

Situation in gulf countries particularly in their small family owned companies is different. They normally start the units with second hand machinery and manage with experienced working supervisory staff, who work with hands on, as these are temporary migrant skilled people, desperate to perform.

They work even two levels low, as salaries are lucrative. So, Core Skilled and hands on experience is very important. I had the opportunity of taking up such two jobs.

The first one was in Sandi Kingdom in a Steel rolling mill, who were considering to set-up a new continuous casting steel melting shop, consisting of electric are furnace and casting. They had technical Quotations of two Indian suppliers to scrutinize and do technical evaluation.

I was also involved in QMS quality management system, as I had been MR- management representative in my previous company in India for 1SO9000 & QS-9000. I could not get my self involved in their regular on going mainstream functions like machinery maintenance, as that department was not a weak area for them, and did nor need strengthening.

Funds for proposed expansion was not available at that point of time and it was expected to start only after two / three years. As QMS was not full time job, so I could not find a permanent placement and had to come back after short time.

Later on, after two years, my assistant here could use his influence to get this job for managing their expansion. A new Mini steel plant was set up and was working well.

Second experience is of steel rod rolling mill in Bahrain, where I got responsibility of Plant in charge and I joined with lot of enthusiasm but soon discovered that they needed only a rolling mill foreman, who would himself personally do the roll pass combination and setting of mill-stands to roll out steel rods within desired tolerance.

As I am not a mill operation person, this assignment also did not go very smoothly. Meanwhile, my visa renewal issue came due to age limit and their government did not allow me to extend my stay there, as I had gone there on my post-retirement.

There are also **successful ventures** which I am sharing here.

First one is of a Ferro Alloys Plant in Bhutan, which I visited repeatedly. Shop floor staff was trained on various aspects of work place organization and equipment care. A two week long training programme was conducted to make the participants confident in handling & maintaining their machines.

This Plant makes Ferro alloys in induction furnaces which consume mainly electric power. 85% of the manufacturing cost is electric energy. Cost of electricity in Bhutan is one fourth of India, as Bhutan has many hydro electric power generating units. They supply Ferro alloys to all Indian steel plants.

Bhutan Locals are not very experienced in Steel industry, so most of the managerial & technical personal are Indians. For making a call from Bhutan on landline in 2010 used to be Rs. 29/=per minute. As I was staying in border town, I could just cross the border to go Indian side Jaigaon & make call to Indian rates. Gates to Jaigaon India closes at 10 P.M & opens at 6 A.M. so no road connection to India during night time.

Other one was of visit to Lagos, Nigeria, where I went for conducting training Programme for 30 Plant managers on Plant machinery maintenance.

Again, recently I went for my second visit to Lagos, Nigeria, where I went for conducting six Manufacturing Plants' Equipment Health Audit. This group of Companies is owned by Indian Residents of Nigeria. Once you enter these Plants, you would find Indian Environment and Hindi working language. Even food served in their Canteens is all Indian. Even Chef and Cooks have been trained to cook Indian Food.

Unit Head, Sectional Incharge and Key Process technicians are from India. Remaining all Workers are locals who manage Security, Housekeeping, Transportation and all the Workers carrying out all the activities.

– *Moral* –

Some times it is not competence but practical skill is required for tackling technical issues & challenges, particularly for specialised Small enterprises.

Nigeria is land of Opportunities, particularly for Indians settled there.

Chapter 13

Small is Beautiful for Fast Track Growth

Big companies have lot of advantages of volume production but they also have issues due to organizational inertia. All Companies build its own culture and customs and it becomes difficult to change it later on, it can also carry lot of dead wood. Smaller companies are more flexible and more dynamic with faster response.

Experience with two such organizations is being shared here.

The first company was business-family managed going on fast track. The company was hiring the best people in industry to accelerate build up of Projects & plant process with cheapest secondary new equipment and second hand Mainline set ups purchased from abroad at almost scrap price. In many Western countries, old obsolete equipment have no takers and there all get disposed as scarp.

As we all know, new HODs (Departmental Heads) joining with attractive perks are highly motivated and to make good mark, they give their best to set up good systems and processes. After giving their best for 3-4 years, their capacity to continue to make contribution at same rate diminishes. Meanwhile, few of the juniors get personal support of top management, so deserving candidates start leaving the company. Still the organizations keeps prospering as sub-ordinates by that time get trained and become competent & also ready to take up the leadership role.

Many organization have systematic approach to make staff to be self accountable to perform effectively. One of these methods to accomplice "SELF SET TARGETS". Every supervisor has to set number of tasks with targets and at the beginning of each month, and has to make Self - evaluation of achievements and do self marking out of 100 marks. Every supervisor sends these report to HR Department and they maintain its record for scrutiny and reference of management as & when required and also for his promotion and increment during annual assessments, these achievements are compiled by assesses and given to assessor for his consideration.

Let us see the Bigger Companies with many layers of command and number of operating Divisions with many departments. A fresher joins one of the Section of a Department and it takes him number of years to become Sectional Incharge and then only he is visible as some one in the Department. Many ambitious talented persons get frustrated and leave the organization for their personal growth.

Chapter 14

Executive Health, Efficiency & Family Life Challenges

Executive Health is important factors for their alertness and efficiency. For smooth running of the Organization, its officers need to be mentally and physically fit, strong and motivated.

Even Government provides or tries to provide pollution free environment with parks & open Air Gymnasiums and swimming pools & sports grounds.

For plant located in country side, Employers provide outdoor & indoor Games, libraries, Movies, Gyms, Clubs & swimming pools etc. for Employees in their colonies. Basic purpose is keep all the Industrial colony population in healthy living. These are all recharging mechanism essential for growth of all concerned.

In regard to facilities provided, there can be undercharging or overcharging or even discharging of system in extreme cases. A balanced approach helps to maintain a healthy situation.

Outsiders & bystanders may think it to be pampering of the employees' Families to luxury, without understanding the basic necessity of such facilities & infrastructure like regularly receiving & free dropping of passengers to Railway Station & shopping centers for plant located in country side.

We envy Young Professional rising to CEO Level. Cut throat competition has its effect on executive health and their family life. Incentives for results by the organizations are sky high. You can see, many CEO's at very young age with their annual pay package running in many lakhs. These incentives create very high mental & physical pressure for executives to perform to produce results far exceeding management expectations. In the process, their health and family life suffers, as they are always in state of tremendous mental tension along with long working hours & inadequate sleep.

Another aspect is most of Big companies have free treatment for their employees and many of them before retirement go for major correction operations & problems detected, even with treatment abroad. They want to be perfectly fit to lead the post-retirement life, free of these Health issues. They spend lot of company money for their body overhaul before retirement. But it some time creates other problems which would not happened, if they had not disturbed the body system. Sometime, it better for body to take its own course, instead of such interventions, just because it is free or you can afford, without any financial dent.

I know of one of my Defence friends who got one stent and more stents all free with VIP facilities and died prematurely, as one of these stents got displaced.

Now add Family issues of long working hours and being away from the family. Most of the manufacturing plants are normally away from towns in countryside due to Government regulations and incentives are more for these far away places. Taking employment with these Companies leads to relocation of families with compromise on education &

social facilities. If family stays in town and person has long distances to attend to his duty. So, he never sees daylight at home.

Not that management are not aware of these mental stress as professional hazard of their senior executives being under intense work pressure. Many of them are taking action in different ways to help these Executive tackle these factors. Some Companies have health programmes for their employees. Few do physical fitness exercises of employees for 15 minutes at the beginning of the day. Few provide indoor games like Carom Boards & table-tennis which employees can use in their lunch break.

In Employees' Colonies, Gymnasium, swimming pool, & Tennis courts are generously built, free movies show and other social activities so that Employees & their Families remain positively engaged physically & mentally.

– *Lesson* –

Employees Welfare Activities are necessary to Prosperity of the Organizations.

Chapter 15

Leader Integrity & Confidence

In a plant where my friend, Sundar Kumar, was working, Management brought in a new dynamic plant head with good track record. New Boss already had known many of juniors in our plant, who had worked under him in earlier companies. He was, both Technically & managerially competent with good use of computer / laptop, which was not very common in 1998 in manufacturing plants. From day one he was in control, as he had his own reliable channel of information. He liked to involve Sundar Kumar in plant activities, as Sundar Kumar was senior most and engineering head, as for making all the modifications, he needed his support.

Plant at that time had lot of issues with workers with active union activities. The plant was far away from city in village area with lot of workers from near by villages. He involved Sundar Kumar in union matters also and asked him to co-ordinate their discussions.

He provided Sundar Kumar with a Dictaphone, in which all conversation with workers could be recorded for reference. He soon got good grip on the plant operations and wanted to further shows his strength, as he was himself a local person, earlier plant head and top management were all outsiders.

In his haste, he started making changes and taking bold decisions for which his foundation was still not very sound. He had taken lot of new modification projects, in which Sundar Kumar was providing him all the support but he thought of having a separate project cell. Sundar Kumar objected to this change but had to accept as he was already nearing retirement age.

The union president was an operator in maintenance department and Sundar Kumar had been tactfully dealing with him. Now, different HOD was dealing with him and their friction increased. Even in the new situation, plant head depended lot on Sundar Kumar in all important matters, including union dealings.

As the union president was missing mostly from his duty and also neglecting his duty many times, he was issued warning few times and finally, it was decided to issue him a termination letter. Along with personal department head, Sundar Kumar was also consulted regarding this action. Sundar Kumar strongly disagreed and advised them not to precipitate the issue.

As plant head by now had support of many loyal workers, who had previously worked under him and had very strong relationship, he thought that a big group of workers would stand in his support, as & when required. In spite of my repeated appeal to him, he remained adamant, so Sundar Kumar assured him of my support to him, even if it was to get beating by workers. Boss was confident that nothing like that would happen. He took permission from H.O. in city to issue letter to union president. Top management also arranged police protection as stand by. Letter was issued at 4:30 P.M. by the personal department. Sundar Kumar stayed in chief's office, all other HODs were scared and stayed in their office rooms in their areas. Middle and junior staff had already left by 5:45 P.M.

Around 7 P.M., a group of workers entered chief's office and pulled us both Boss & Sundar Kumar of the room and also pulled personal Dept. HOD. This mob started kicking them towards the gate, which is about half an kilometers. All the workers had surrounded the main gate. At the gate, and around place was full of workers crowd, few outsiders also had also joined, meanwhile, police force had also reached and gave beating to few Workers leading the crowd.

Situation became more volatile and even security staff were scared of workers. Some politicians & other Outside unions leader had also reached. Chief was forced to apologize and take back the dismissed letter. Thereafter, the crowd dispersed and they could leave from plant after mid-night around 2 P.M. They went to Police station & primary Health Centre, as Top management had arranged for FIR & medical examination. Case was filed in the court.

Later on top management sent a fact finding agency to investigate and their confidential report was in workers favour. So, Chief left the company and went aboard to join a new company.

To avoid any complication of pending court case, while doing foreign job, he came back and with management permission withdrew the case, stating that no such incidence happened. Court readily closed the case.

– *Moral* –

While dealing with Workers, you need lot of Patience & Tact, even if You may be very good in your work and may have lot of support.

Chapter 16

Formula of Chinese Quality & Productivity

Everyone knows so much about Chinese Quality & productivity, so I do not have to discuss & explain it all. Why Chinese have captured world market and why Chinese products are cheapest. Why all big brand names of USA have outsourced production of their products to Chinese plants or have established their manufacturing facility in China.

Presently I am sharing some of my observations, based on personal experience during my visit around two decades back, in connection with purchase Agency of ball & roller bearings and its accessories. I visited a town in south in china, called Dalian, this is also called bearing town, as all the plants in this town only make bearings and its accessories. They have their own training institutes in the Town which impart knowledge on bearing technology.

One time it is used to agriculture village but over a period, even the villagers got trained into Technical & Engineering works. Even some of the farmer families have installed even CNC turning machines in their modified Residential cattle sheds. Husband & wife both operate CNC machines, as they get its training in institute nearby. On one side, they have poultry, other side cattle shed and inside building, they have CNC shaft turning machines, all in the same compound. So they are able to run small scale home industry, almost at nominal investment.

Most of the Manufacture suppliers keep three grades, one is the special grade with world class quality, second is normal as per market demand and third is cheap to beat the pricing elsewhere. You choose and you get it, If the plant is ISO 9000 certified, their certifying agency audits are quite strict. In one of the plant, I liked the product and its finish but my Chinese interpreter and advisor prevented me to place my order on this supplier. He advised me that I could depend only on ISO 9000 certified Suppliers, as they were transparent and would follow the contract terms. Other suppliers may not dispatch their deliveries, same item matching the sample which was approved.

Female employees were encouraged to take up jobs, matching their skill & calibre. While going on national highways, we found even in mid-night, that all the toll plaza were being operated only by females. Only few male security guards were present for their Security.

Even Economy budget hotels are also well equipped with good facilities and service. While taking my morning tea on tenth floor hotel room balcony, when I looked outside, I found number of families- Gents, ladies & children, all doing exercise in open gymnasium. This was the scene there two decades back now, of course, Now even in our country such facilities are widely available and becoming popular.

– Lesson –

Public Awareness and Innovation plays key role. Understanding Customers' need by Consistent dedicated Hard working people with suitable planning & Government encouragement can bring prosperity for its citizens.

Chapter 17

"Self Certified Small Manufacturing Units"

Major Auto manufacturing companies making world class cars & other vehicles are now following JIT - *just in time* delivery system where in the components supply is received daily or even shift wise in some cases, when Vendors are near by. Auto Components received are directly taken to production assembly line and fitted on the vehicle frame. Statically Random samples are taken from every lot and are sent for offline inspection. You must have read in Newspaper about Automobiles Recall System. If any defect reaches customer or found during the component inspection, vehicles are recalled for correction / replacement of component. This is a standard practice, followed by Auto Industry world wide.

Case No. 1:
Long back, Proprietor of one such small unit in Kolhapur approached me to implement ISO 9000- Quality management system in their workshop and wanted me only, as he felt that their unit could benefit from my experience, although my professional rate was costlier.

I worked with them for few years to establish all the systems, work instruction, standard operating procedures and also trained their staff.

They were ancillary product suppliers to Tata motors for their passenger cars and had to undergo regular product and process second Party Audit by the customer. On successful assessment, this supplier got approval as being self-certified vendor. They performed well in their product deliveries with zero defect even for over two years. The unit was doing well and they were expanding their business.

Case No. 2:

Two decade back, one small stainless steel fabricator making special equipment wanted to make their ISO 9000 system to be more effective as they were interested in getting benefit of this certification. I got associated with them, but unit was very small, with only eight workers and four engineers, although their M.D. was qualified & very competent engineer, and it also had two more Director (Later on one of senior director retired.), one for finance & marketing and other for family friend who was helping in investment and infra-structure support. Their Workshop was in small shed with M.D. sitting in one corner.

M.D. was always looking for new ideas and we used to do lot of brain-storming, how to improve Quality & Delivery and increase units output. Units working system was very old, all manual activities, time consuming methodology. To get even the centre point of disc flange, they would use very time consuming method of geometry box type jumbo campus to draw arcs and its intersections. I introduced the concept of Jigs & fixtures for quick marking of jobs to machined or drilled. Later on, they themselves developed many Jigs & fixture devices for tilting & turning of jobs for doing welding on jobs, to improve productivity and quality of welding.

Skill matrix evaluation was done on later stage, when work force had increased to over forty employees on role and equal number on contract. Production Turnover increased from less than half crore to over seven crores. Company moved into regular big shed with overhead crane facility, radioactive testing & shot-blasting machine, acid pickling facility for cleaning. Welders were trained for doing boiler quality welding and also got certificate from boiler inspectorate.

By now, Unit had standard working system, with more than ten supervisor with works General manager with proper store, purchase, design & quality department which was required to satisfy third party inspection for overseas dispatches and prestigious customers.

Their products by now in demand world wide. They got dedicated bulk supply order from foreign company which booked full capacity of existing Plant on long term contract. Therefore, they went for second much bigger unit to meet demand of their existing customers. This also made it possible to manage ownership issue. Between two of them, they divided their ownership so that there is no difficulty is faced by younger generation.

I am still called once a while to advise them to tackle any technical or organisational challenges. Company has also the satisfaction of having trained many fine engineers who have left them to make good careers elsewhere with big companies.

I call this Managing Director as an institution itself for High Tech. stainless steel fabrication and have been pursuing him to set a training centre for employees skill up gradation.

– Moral –

If Systems are built and sincerely followed, even Small companies can easily give exceptionally good results, They do need Competent advisors / consultants and should be ready to take actions based on their Guidance.

Chapter 18

"When Should You Hire a Technical Consultant"

As adequate technical expertise and industry experience is generally not available in-house, many companies hire technical consultants to improve productivity and skill up gradation of their employees. Utilization and effectiveness depends on many factors, including the internal team interacting and coordinating activities of the consultant & Employees Response. I will share my personal experience with few companies.

Some have the mind set that the consultant collects information and data, available with shop floor staff and based on it, gives recommendations of actions but solutions are already known to them. There is nothing which plant employees do not knows as they are running plant for long time. Anyway, in such cases, action plans are made with responsibility and target dates. In many cases, even the tasks given are done but substantial benefits are not achieved. At the end of the contract, all in such organizations agree that this consultant was no good and look for another one.

Then they discontinue hiring, because top management is made to believe by the plant team that they are good or better than the consultant. The company's ambitions to grow faster are delayed.

In some cases, local management subject consultant to go through many tests and give them task/ assignments which they knows are not feasible. In the process, consultant surrenders and runs away as he cannot perform and give them desired results. Consultant gets no co-operation but only lip concurrence.

There are cases, when the plant local Team is excited to get the opportunity of technical expertise availability at shop-floor and shares their bottlenecks and challenges and also explains about various actions previously taken by them to resolve yhe problems. In such cases, the technical consultant with experience and knowledge is able to coach & guide them to under take corrective measures.

I will narrate one such case. Around 2005, one of the reputed Tyre company was going for TS 16949- Auto industry QMS (quality management system) certification to meet Auto customers' requirement. This system standard specifies that plant should and effective Predictive maintenance practice. They gave me the contract to establish it in their plants both in Mumbai and other town. They have about 3500 employees in one plant and around 2000 in other plant. I provided training to over 1500 employees for their skill upgradation.

Shop floor total plant maintenance practices for equipment care in both plants were reviewed & revised. A 100 page Predictive maintenance manual was prepared. Earlier forms & formats and P.M. (preventive maintenance) checklists were different for both, these were standardised, so that reports of all key parameters are prepared and in the same format. One completion of the task, their V.P. operation congratulated me for this achievement.

I have to thank both the plant heads for their co-operation and support, which made the implementation smooth and satisfying.

Scene in all plants is not same, although top management expectation are similar.

One such experience was in one Steel Plant, where operation & maintenance heads did not want any outsider to take credit. So although long list of suggestions and action plans were made, on the ground the implementation was not effective. So, it was a case of lower gains.

One advise I give to colleagues is not to do plant maintenance & equipment health Audit, because plant local management will always challenge the finding and you may not be invited for further assignments.

Chapter 19

"ISO 9000 & QS-16949 – Implementation & Certification"

My another Friend, Abhay Kumar shared his experience. Around 1997 end, his management decided to go for ISO 9000 - quality management system. As this type of activity is generally managed by QA (quality assurance) department, QA head was requested to initiate it but QA head considered it too time consuming, he declined to take this responsibility.

Although as head of engineering & maintenance, Abhay had much wider area to manage, management approached him to take up this responsibility, along with regular work and they wanted the certification soon, as most of the customers had been demanding that our plant operation to be meeting ISO 9000 requirements.

No one in plant had any knowledge about its requirements. As the company was very tight on funds, they had to do in much cheaper manner. Abhay selected two engineers to assist himself in its documentation. Staff was trained and work instructions, departmental procedures were prepared, he got guidance from our sister unit, as they already had ISO 9000 certification.

Making the shop floor staff to prepare documentation and maintaining records was big challenge. The staff started asking the management whether they would their departmental jobs or do ISO 9000 paper work. However, they could make small group in every department interested and company successfully passed final Audit by the third party certification body and got the certification, followed by big celebrations.

While getting recommended for three year certificate, M.D. announced that company must have TS 16949 certificate also, as Auto manufacturing customers were demanding our company to meet this standard.

Again, the team there had no knowledge of this QS-9000 - new QMS systems but he said one year was deadline. They were left on our own to learn and upgrade QMS to QS-9000 (as TS16949 was called QS-9000 before 2000). They attended training programmes & obtained necessary documents from Indian standards offices.

That time, Abhay recalled of having met, during his visit to Jamshedpur to one Industrial Plant, one representative of certification agency, Nathan & Nathan Certification consultancy with their base in Bangalore. Abhay managed to contact them and with their support started the implementation.

In our Plant, Cross – functional teams were formed to address various requirements of the standard and about eight months passed while implementing various Documented Procedures.

Meanwhile, Another mini steel plant, which was also preparing for it ahead of them, went for certification audit but failed in their effort as they got many N.C's - non conformance in Final Audit (some say 32 nos). This information had very demoralizing effect on his colleagues in that Plant, as few of the officers had previously worked there & respected that company's system.

All the senior persons in plant wanted that they should defer Certification schedule of third party for pre-audit, as they were likely to get still more N.C.s.

Under this environment, before next management review meeting was conducted by M.D., Abhay briefed M.D. that he should appreciate effort of all the department and tell them that he has found that plant was fully prepared for the audit. He boosted morale of all.

That was in 1999 in around Sept and he said by 26 Jan 2000, he is sure company will have the certificate. The same thing happened, all the staff at grass- root level put their best and plant had its QS-9000 certificate on 23-1-2000, as there were only two minor NCs in the final audit and certification body auditors were happy with their findings. It was perhaps the first mini steel plant at that time to get this certification.

Their sister unit too needed this certification urgently but they were still struggling to sustain their basic 1SO 9000. So Abhay was assigned to visit the other Plant to guide them in starting implementation of QS-9000.

As Abhay was to soon retire, Abhay provided them initial start up support. Other plants also gained the courage for this certificate. Other steel plant near by requested his directors for help and their whole QMS team gathered in H.O. in Pune to get guidance tips from Abhay on how to satisfy QS 9000 standard requirements.

After his retirement, they invited him to take the assignment for their implementation. They assured to issue W.O. (work order) of contract soon but after some time Abhay was informed that few top level changes were taking so he should wait.

After few months, Abhay visited again to find a completely new team to replace all old people who had served there for 15-20 years. With new team, many new challenges came up.

Finally, Abhay was given contract of improving their plant maintenance and increasing reliability of their EOT Cranes (over head travelling of cranes) operation, in particular.

– Moral –

If Management puts trust and support Plant personnel, great results & Targets can be achieved.

Chapter 20

TPM Companies Culture & OPL – One Point Lesson

I am sure by now, you all must have got the opportunity to visit some TPM Companies. What is a TPM company. Difference between a world class company and a traditional company. When you enter the security gate of a TPM company, you can notice the difference, the things & place is organized and set method & procedures of their working. TPM company has different culture, you will look forward to working for, though every company has its own distinct culture.

Around two decades back, I had the privilege of visiting two TPM units of a Soap making Company -one in Rajpura in Punjab near Ambala & second one in Khamgaon near Jalgaon in Maharashtra. Both the units make Soaps, one makes Pears and other variety.

Not going into details, I just share the catering facility- we were served lunch in Japanese style- sitting on the floor with food inThali on a bench /chauki. They had free tea/coffee machine Counter in a common place, where employees could go anytime, if they wanted additional serving, in addition to regular tea/snacks served by the company.

Motivational slogans are displayed all over, beside technical & performance information. Social together & competition photos of employees & families are also displayed.

Innovation & Kaizen benefits are separately shared. During plant round in khamgaon unit plant, we noticed two big empty sheds full of shelves. On enquiry, came to know that Pears soap cakes earlier needed a curing period of 42 days, during this period soap cakes were stored in these shelves. With Innovation & technology breakthrough research, curing period is now only 48 hours, so those two sheds were not required and These were out of use. There is special emphasis on waste control. My visit was to conduct a training workshop on converting "wealth from waste".

TPM culture is transforming many companies where Autonomous maintenance initiative to make machine operators to do self initiated equipment care is also implemented.

One point lesson [OPL] is also part of TPM and many companies are taking good benefit by practicing it. I found in one Oil making company plants also having very effective OPL system. In one corner of the hall, they have displayed all do's & don'ts, pictorials method of doing it correctly and these are also put up in plant offices. It takes long time to build company culture even with active involvement of top management being role model and setting up stage. Employees at all level are trained continuously to upgrade & update themselves.

Small group activities with workers level involvement and empowerment, base is prepared to achieve also self certified competent & confident motivated lower level employees.

They can also form Quality Circles (QC) for employees' small group to take up improvement projects for solving problems at your shop-floor. There is established procedure to systematically find out solutions, implement it and finally make management presentation of benefits derived.

For conducting training, during my visits to Blue Chip Companies, I found Guest houses & Bhavans named specially with slogans & styles, corporate take pride of naming their VIP guest houses with their product or company names.

I am sharing few here names of Guest Houses in Various Companies. SAIL-Steel authority of India limited calls them Guest houses-Roukela House, Bhillai house., Burnpur house.

Essar Hazira, Gujarat, has excellence training centre named as Briquette House, their complex in Barbil, kohinjhar as Ore house & refinery of Esser in jam nagar is OIL house.

HEG making electrodes in Bhopal have it Graphite House. Hindalco has their Kolkata training centre as White House. Many Companies has good slogans & gods statues also.

Many places have lot of slogans-both motivational & classic slogan all over plant and their employees colony. All TPM practicing companies also slogans widely used all over.

QCFI, Quality circle forum of India, regularly Arranges national level competitions for recognize good work being done by quality circle teams in various companies to encourage more employees to join this initiative.

What is the difference between a traditional Indian company and a world class company. Traditional companies spend time and resources on non productive repetitive routine preventive maintenance activities, where as world class companies do more on modification and equipment improvement activities, this reducing need less routine activities.

For example, if a A-40 V-belt needs to be replaced every three month, but it can be replaced by B-40/C-40 V-belt by modifying the belt-pulley, increases the life of V-belt to over one year, so reducing need for frequent replacement. If a hose pipe fails frequently can be modified by better pressure rating & better specification to again increases its life.

There are so many improvement possibilities in every plant.

– Lesson –

Endless improvement possibilities in every plant to become a better Company, a journey towards world class company.

Chapter 21

KPI (Key Parameters Indicators) & EVA – Economics Value Addition

There are two type of activities in Production process - non value adding & value adding. EVA-Economic value Addition is the main objective of any process.

In corporate world, employees' when annual assessment is done, one of the factor is to how much EVA- economic value addition, he is making. Management want consistently good performance, but only robots & machines can do it. Employees are humans and their productivity varies with time, situation & moods.

Their motivations also change with situation and length of service.

1. A new employees is highly motivated but least effective as he has to learn the job.
2. Then in short period, he becomes very effective along with being motivated.
3. Over a period, motivation becomes low, as he is not complemented continually and loses motivation.
4. Finally, he is neither effective nor motivated and the right choice of being considered as surplus person in the group for VRS (voluntary retirement) or dismissal.

No one can live on past Glory, So it necessary for every one to regularly keep performing all the time by adding economic value. In this way, he will grow in organization as well as in his personality.

Prior to getting job, fresher's keep learning courses on their parents' money. When in employment, person gets opportunity to learn by understanding the working systems and may be do some part time learning or doing some courses to develop his skills & knowledge. Even part time MBA courses are available.

Basically, it depends on the number of hours one can put for professional work. Some time, commuting to work place covering long distances, even in company's transport, can be big time waster. Lucky are people, you stay near work place and use extra time saved productively.

Being cost conscious very important, Everywhere, there are opportunities for savings by having an analytical approach. There are many management tools which can be used, like Kaizen, Quality Circle, Suggestion box and seven QC tools.

Both small group and individual improvement projects can be encouraged with rewards and appreciations.

Data compiling and trend monitoring can be reference to track performance. KPI- key parameter indicators are also used to monitor performance. More than ten type standards KPI are available like cost / unit, consumption/hour, cycle time. In many, companies, daily income and expense record is maintained to calculate, profit/loss.

There was strong monitoring system with incentives and penalties according to group and individual performance. This was done by regular KPI – key parameters indicators performance measurement, based on percentage achievement level.

Every month, performance based on KPI is measured. There is standard Chart, and based on assessment bonus and penalty are given to all individual. Performance Measurement can be Individual or for the Team.

Employees Skill matrix evaluation is done periodically and section wise and level wise average was displayed on noticeboard for further improvements. Training and Development plan for each Officer is prepared.

– *Moral* –

For survival & growth of a commercial unit, EVA- economic value addition at all level and by all is an important factor to monitor, for controlling & taking timely action.

Chapter 22

How to Face JOB INTERVIEWs – TIPS

Proper preparation for interview is vital for selection. Beside regular coaching & training, few tips which can help the candidate, are shared here.

First is knowing the job requirement and impressing on the interviewers that you are most suitable person for the job. While replying various questions, candidate can to indicate how his competence will be useful for the company.

There is a very popular example of a boy who went to get a job in an antique Selling Shop. While he was waiting, he had toothpick to clean his teeth, there was a customer there, thinking him to be salesman the customer enquired from him what was he holding in his hand. by stating that Tooth Pick, he holding was used by Napoléon Budapest.

The Boy was immediately taken for Sales person job, even without interview.

Job Interview Tips:
Sanjay Shaarthi had Divya Drishti – Auto Distance Vision. While Duryodhan was taking interview for Horse Rath (chariot) of his Father, blind king, Thritrashtra for a Sarthi – Chariot driver

Sanjay could have put his trump card, along with driving the chariot expertise, that he could also make the kings see through him, as he describe Events taking place even at distant places.

So, He being the most suitable person he got the job. If you too can put fourth a strong plus point of your competence, which would be of use for the company, job will be yours

Other true example, there was boy, working in weighing machine company. After suitable coaching & advice, during interview, he impressed the interviewer that he could use his electronic experience & knowledge for improvement and modifications in their plant. He offered to fix load cells on various EOT (electric over head cranes) cranes. This company had number of Cranes and wanted to improve Cranes utilization. They were satisfied and he got the job.

He was quite ambitious and was also doing part time study. Later on he took unauthorized long break and was dismissed. As he did not have another job, so he kept begging for reinstatement of his job. Plant head was kind person, so he agreed to give him fresh appointment effective from fresh date of issue of letter.

Personality, discipline & showing keenness to give results also helps. Description of past achievements and how positively candidate solved problems also a good factor.

You can describe your weakness also in a positive way, like you are inpatient, indicating that once a project in undertaken, his colleagues may take it in normal course but you are very particular about the deadline & quality of work, so you put your heart & head to achieve it in best possible way.

Answer can be "I find it difficult to say no to others, straight away that it can be done or it is impossible but I ask for time so that I can find out whether there is method to meet the challenge".

Surprisingly, in many case, there is an out of box solution possible. I do enjoy such victories.

I will like to share an example of out of box (lateral thinking) thinking process.

Story of Two Pebbles Lateral Thinking

There was an old person under heavy debts which he was unable to pay the Shrewd Money lender, who made an offer to old man that he would write off all his debts, if the man would let him marry his daughter.

So he proposed a bargain.

He said he would forgo the debt if he could marry his daughter. Both the farmer and his daughter were horrified by the proposal. So the cunning money-lender suggested that they let providence decide the matter. He told them that he would put a black pebble and a white pebble into an empty money bag. Then the girl, would have to pick one pebble from the bag.

1. If she picked the black pebble, she would become his wife and her father's debt would be forgiven.
2. If she picked the white pebble she need not marry him and her father's debt would still be forgiven.
3. But if she refused to pick a pebble, her father would be thrown into jail.

Finely, They were standing on a pebble strewn path in the farmer's field. As they talked, the moneylender bent over to pick up two pebbles. As he picked them up, the sharp-eyed girl noticed that he had picked up two black pebbles and put them into the bag. He then asked the girl to pick a pebble from the bag.

Now, imagine that you were standing in the field. What would you have done if you were the girl?

If you had to advise her, what would you have told her?

Careful analysis would produce three possibilities:
1. She should refuse to take a pebble.
2. The girl should show that there were two black pebbles in the bag and expose the money-lender as a cheat.
3. The Girl should pick a black pebble and sacrifice herself in order to save her father from his debt and imprisonment.

Take a moment to ponder over the story. The above story is used with the hope that it will make us appreciate the difference between lateral and logical thinking. The girl's dilemma cannot be solved with traditional logical thinking. Think of the consequences if she chooses the above logical answers.

What would you recommend that she should do?
Well, here is what she did…

The girl put her hand into the moneybag and drew out a pebble. Without looking at it, she fumbled and let it fall onto the pebble-strewn path where it immediately became lost among all the other pebbles.

"Oh, how clumsy of me," she said. "But never mind, if you look into the bag for the one that is left, you will be able to tell which pebble I picked." Public was all watching the show.

Since the remaining pebble is black, it must be assumed that she had picked the white one. And since the money-lender dared not admit his dishonesty, the girl changed what seemed an impossible situation into an extremely advantageous one.

Summary:

Most complex problems do have a solution.

It is only that we don't attempt to think.

She had out of Box Thinking capability of Lateral Thinking. Answer is obvious and she could get free because of her lateral thinking.

Another Example,

There is always a different way to see things- which can be positive or negative.

One person had magic dog, who could walk over water but his companion was always with negative attitude, commented that his dog even does not know how to swim.

One other *example of positive attitude* is they say people throw bricks on you, but these can be used in making a building.

Then we talk of real & apparent.

In one colony, police men used to visit a particular house quite often. Neighbours discussed that some thing unlawful is being done by them and they were avoiding this occupant.

But One day that occupant distributed sweets to all neighbours with the news that their son has been promoted to inspector of police.

– Moral of the Story –

Planning of work and sharpening of Skill is vital. Where Traditional Thinking does not work, Thinking capability of Lateral Thinking can provide Solution.

Also, Important to understand difference between apparent & real truth

Chapter 23

"Obedient Vs. Smart Employees and Leadership Styles"

Ever wondered who is better obedient or smart Employees to work for you.

The obedient Employee reaches work place before time and surely works full day to do all the assigned jobs, even stays late to clear backlogs He never gives to chance to complain for any non –compliance you like him and he is your favourite person.

On the other hand, other person questions the merit of doing a job and debates but once he accepts any task, he does it in best possible manner. He difficult to handle and not a good Team Member but full of ideas. He works by clock and is out at 5 P.M even without asking you.

Whom would you prefer in your area. How to decide this now, traditionally you would have you been given preference to obedient Employee, it may not be easy but then are few factors which need to be considered, while making such decision. Every shop have various activities, including many routine repetitive type jobs to be done for smooth running of the system, like Preventive Maintenance compliance and minor recurring activities. These can be done best by obedient nature staff, as they are willing to do task as per the need of time and derive satisfaction by the quantity of jobs, they have performed.

Then there are many challenging tasks and problems with no visible solution, smart people enjoy experimenting to find solutions and to feel Hero's that they have successfully completed a difficult Task, provided they are often recognized for their contributions.

The point is there are different Tasks under different conditions which require different characteristic of the performer. Once you understand it and assign them as their aptitude, you will be able to best utilise their capabilities.

Along with this, situational Leadership style can get best results from them.

Employees can be divided in different groups
1. Supervisors, who need to be given detailed work instruction for most of the jobs.
2. People, who know their job well and you just need to tell them the requirement.
3. People, along with performing quality work, can guide their co-workers to follow the right procedure.

There are few with negative approach who do not it well themselves and even spoil other good workers For them doing work is evil, they think more of their rights and less of their duties & responsibilities They are parasite and removing them is generally the only solution. application of Theory 'X' is applicable for them, that is fear factor, stick & carrots. This was management practice followed in olden times.

Then Theory 'Y' followed, which believed that employees can be motivated to perform well with coaching and suitable guidance. Further to that came, Theory 'Z' with Employees involvement and empowerment for superior results.

Some believe in classifying the population on the concept of theory described in book Brave New World written long time back by Aldus Huxley, it divides the people in different categories, Alpha, Beta, Gamma & Delta. Alpha are superior class, like blue eyed boys, which governs the society, Betas are supporting, the performers, who operate the system & responsible for productive & sustainable actions. Then are Gamma' s & Deltas who are used as servant class to carry out grass root, labour class, duties.

These people are programmed accordingly, even earlier in the mother's womb so that their mind-set is ready to think as per their category. Virtual entertainment systems are provided for them to experience joy of a Virtual Holiday trips though these advanced Technologies. We find many of these points actually happening today, all though these points have been described by the Authors long back half the century earlier.

– *Moral* –

Any organization is made up with people with different competence and mind-set, it is up to Management personnel, how to get best results through them. No single formula & guideline can be prescribed.

Chapter 24

"World Class Maintenance – WCM System"

World class Maintenance means Zero Breakdown, Zero Accident and zero Defect. These are all are performance Parameters of any manufacturing Plant. But more important is WCM Mind-set culture, where every shop floor staff in the organization operates with the help of WCM Management Tools & Techniques.

They practice Pro-Active Maintenance strategy, which is the Best strategy, where Plant Equipment is divided in three Categories:

1) Equipment failing suddenly without previous Warning – where Failure is Non-Predictable

2) Equipment Failure is generally Predictable, as its failure is normally Age Related

3) CBM- where Equipment health is measured by CBM- Condition Based Monitoring Techniques and Instruments so that Rate of deterioration can be found.

Different Type of Maintenance strategies need to be practiced on for different equipment, as only one type of Maintenance practice cannot prevent failure in all type of Equipment.

For Equipment failing based on its normal Aging pattern can be best attended by *Preventive maintenance* by making a calendar based schedule with suitable PM checklist.

Equipment with unpredictable Failure characteristic should be permitted to run till Failure, as no Maintenance Action can prevent its Failure.

In such cases, standby Equipment option can be used or a developing a parallel operating system with multiple smaller Capacity Equipment so that one of many operating provides time for failed machine repair or replacement.

For regular Repetitive jobs, *Formula one type Pit stop Maintenance* Practice with SMED (single Minute Exchange of Die) approach can be followed to save time and Manpower resources.

For Better Machine upkeep, Autonomous Maintenance is practiced where the Operator take care to attend minor jobs on his machine. This reduces work load pressure on Maintenance staff. This practice is called *TPM - Total productive Maintenance* which Excellent Results of Zero Breakdown, Zero Accident and zero Defect. This TPM Practice involves total company with all employees along with 5-5 Good workplace organization. Recommended that all the Plant should adopt this Practice.

These are five levels of Preventive Maintenance achieved over a period. Once a reasonably good level is achieved, to ensure effectiveness Root cause Analysis and FMEA (Failure Mode Effect Analysis) can be practiced. Instead of assuming that all the Equipment follow standard Bath Tube Failure Pattern with Infant Mortally Random Failure and old Age Trend, A study of actual Failure Pattern is done.

It does not end here. These are still other Approaches with include

a. *CMMS*- Stand alone - Computerized Maintenance Management system with Maintenance software to provide data & Trends information to improve implementation on shop floor by better Monitoring & Recording and Trend Management.

b. *"Tribology study"* with the purpose of preventing Machine Failure by going beyond lubrication practice, to include study of wear and Frication & other Factors, which can not controlled only by Machine lubrication only like Bearing failure due to electrical pitting.

c. *Terotechnology study* involves life-cycle cost studies with interaction between Designers and operation personnel of the Equipment to improve its cost effective utilization.

d. *Pro –Active Maintenance Practice –*

This is an upgrade of Preventive & Predictive Maintenance level by setting higher achievable standards and establishing methods and procedure to achieve these and finally measuring the parameters set earlier.

This Leads to making Maintenance a Profit activity instead of cost activity. Many companies are now adopting this system. This also includes taking up *Equipment life enhancing activities* by examining campaign life of all the component of the Assembly. This study is to locate which components or Sub-assembly do not match the periodic overhaul interval say 2/3 years. New upgraded components, with revised specification or design, are fitted to match or exceed its life to the overhaul period.

For example a V- Belt A-44 may be prematurely failing every six months, the system can be redesigned to fit a B-44 / C- 44 by increasing pulley groove size or having two A-44 V- belts on the pulley with two grooves, depending on what is more convenient under the situation.

These options are easy but are missed out in actual working of huge equipment network of plant system.

e. *Standardization* – is required in every plant as you may be using components of various brand Names and each one has its unique dimensions and are not interchangeable with other brand products, so extra inventory has to be maintained. Once these are standardized on one or two brand, others can be phased off.

f. *Varity Reduction:*

This involves reducing the Range of grades sizes of various consumables like Lubricants and V- Belts and Electrical Contactors.

A plant-wise survey study is done to reduce the Varity of sizes & variety to make it more manageable

For example A company may be using three types of lubricant greases - lithium base, sodium & calcium base. They decide to stock only lithium base grade which being superior to other grades. This makes it easy for plant personnel to handle less number of Lubricant grades.

World class Maintenance can be achieved only by Technical application of these systems and Manpower Role are the key factors. Motivated competent Qualified personnel with good work culture.

This requires skill matrix Evaluation and good work culture but these are time taking activities and you need to have patience to develop them in your organization.

Continuous Training activity for Employees Development is also essential. This covers functional areas. organization behavioural & ISO - QMS Quality Management systems. Again need based learning as per departments requirement has to be included,

Besides this *OPL- One Point Lesson, Kaizen and Practicing Pokayoke* Mistake – proofing Techniques are great improvement Tools.

Plant modification and continuous upgradation activities are must. There is no end to improvements which can be done at work place but active involvement of direct down the line work force Employees is vital, as all the ideas for solution and information of potential problems & failure can be searched and found with their participation.

Employees' Quality Circle _QC Teams for voluntary initiative is essential. Employees & Teams recognitions by Top Management can be big Moral booster.

– *Moral* –

WCM- World class Maintenance is achievable, though it is tough journey. First is Top Management commitment as it requires competent coaching & Training with WCM Tools & techniques, which can be implemented, while simultaneously building company culture.

Chapter 25

"Few Case Studies & Corporate Anecdotes"

There are many interesting cases of various interactions between the Employees & Their Seniors. Few are being narrated here to understand the industrial Work Environment.

First I am taking incidence of *A fly in* vegetable Curry *in company canteen*, Employees Union took a dish from canteen to complain to management that there was a in fly in the vegetable Curry. Canteen Superintendent was summoned and he looked in the dish, he picked up and swallowed the black item with the Comment that it was only black Ellaychi spice, why so much fuss.

Every one in the hall was stunt with surprise & no one any words to comment. The matter is immediately dropped. That is called handling situation with out of Box solution.

In other case, there was Complaint against an elderly Parsee Boss that he called *people SOB (Son of Bitch),* he was summoned by management and warned that he would be punished, if he again calls any one SOB. Next day, he called that person as SOM (Son of a Man) and also told him "Hope you understand what I mean".

Many Bosses have Chamcha employees, who keep praising the Boss and these chamchas promise doing their fellow

Employees of favours to get their application on approved. They do take commission money from them for getting their job done. Sometime, Boss gets complaint against them. In one such case, the chancha employee accepted that he had taken money. but then went on to explain further that on Boss's Birthday, he had brought big flower Bouquet and expensive Gift, he said that he being a poor fellow had to arrange funds for this, so he accepted money given to him, although he never made a demand for it. Boss had forgiven him with a warning not to do in future.

Misusing official position: Once a Head clerk of Boss normally maintaining file of *Department Interviews Records* of Employee workers for Efficiency Trade Tests. People used to bribe him to influence Panel to pass them. As he would already know, who had passed, he would accept bribe and say that he had used his influence to pass the candidate, others who were falling, he would not accept or return before the result was announced saying that Boss did not agree in spite of his recommendation.

Department some times would get bad name for no fault of the Panel members.

Another Case – once *Marketing Department* gets an enquiry for a very big project, and after consulting with concerned departments, concludes that the Company did not have the expertise to execute such project. They are ready to inform the client their inability to send offer for this project.

On getting this information, CEO over rides every one and sends communication to customer that their company has the special Expertise and Technology to undertake such projects and would be glad to execute this project.

Simultaneously, he forms a Task force Team to build up capability for this product service. Finally, the project was completed with flying colours & celebrated in company.

This is the reason that today CEO's of many companies get exceptionally high pay packages. They know that capability of an Organization is limited by the imagination boundary of its people. so what is required is someone to lead them to greater heights. They are able inspire their people to get extraordinary results from team of ordinary people, with suitable management Tools but role of committed people is vital.

In other situation, Employees congratulated CEO on his *new car gifted to CEO by management*. He thanks them for their good work and assured them, if they continued to work sincerely like this, next year, he would surely get a BMW imported Car. This is how our Corporate World operates.

There *two way to rise in an organization*, one is to have all dummies under you so that you become indispensible Hero. The other one is to upgrade & develop Key people so that the organization grows much bigger and you become the group Head.

We have example of few blue chip companies whose management acquired many small enterprises with the support of team work strategies and their management being run by group chairman.

Here are few Corporate Anecdotes being shared.

When Boss says let us make it 'fifty fifty",

All we employees are happy but what is the meaning of 'fifty fifty". It means, Boss will keep 50% and balance 50% will be distributed amongst all group of employees.

When Boss says all the persons who are agreeing to raise hands. then later on he explains to them that they are just being given chance to gracefully respectfully agree, otherwise he has already made up his mind.

Sometimes, *Boss Says* – *"Please do* this for me, then he explains that he says so because of his learning habits & education in Premier Institute, where even the Principal / Director calls students we due respect. Boss Clarifies that staff Should not get confused that they have an option to say No but to do what Boss says, "you bloody well do, whatever you have been asked to do".

One M.D. asks Plant Head to rate his own Annual Appraisal, as Plant Head had great sense of humour, he rated himself poorly in most the areas, with the *concluding Remark* "Fittest person to head the Plant.

Chapter 26

Shop-floor Jobs Vs. Smart Caretakers in Real Estate World

How much a shop-floor supervisor with Technical Skills earns vs. Watchmen Families in Housing Societies?

In construction industry, watchmen /security guards are required from day one for every building for guarding the construction material, so a small cabin is erected in which mostly a migrant family have its Shelter. Some of such watchmen, though illiterate, are smart and resourceful. I am telling you story of one such family.

Of course, as we know, all the members of these migrant family work, we can call them self employed population. Beside normal duty, they even manage to have secondary income, most of the watermen do car washing early in morning and later during the day, do small task for some occupants.

In Cities & Metro Towns, For bachelors & working couples, they do domestic work, their female members even cooking for them.

For Cooking for one time per day, monthly charges are five to seven thousand and for both time is around or more than ten thousand. So even one family member is able to earn around rwenty thousand per month.

They educate their children in good schools for better future, because they get opportunity to stay in the environment of educated Society.

Some set up Tea / snacks and small tiffin / meals outlets in these secluded places to cater to floating population of construction workers.

As more watchmen and domestic help are required, they get them from their native place, may be taking one month salary brokerage, provide them shelter in their cabin for transit period and introduce them for ready jobs coming up with each family moving into new Buildings. Over a period, they have built their community and captured small business of Vegetable & fruit Vendors, tea shop and also of sales boys & girls working in shops, Malls & Parlours.

They can even become sub-brokers for property Sale & rental. People get to know from fellow watchmen by paying nominal amount the owner and thus bypass the Brokers.

Many smart families are earning well and with Savings from here, they are buying land and assets in their native place.

On the other hand, few of children of so called upper middle class are found to be wasting their time in Coffee / Tea joints or roadside gossips. These children leave for their schools early or miss to spend their day wandering around with their friends. As working parents are busy in resolving their professional challenges, their children feel neglected and start getting involved in antisocial activities There are many people around to misguide them and lure them to perform small errand or illegal task for peanuts.

Chapter 27

Attitude Matters & Negative People – WE NEVER Did This WAY

Not all the affluent upper middle class perform poorly, many of them work hard to reach top positions. We blame parenting but there are many other factors, too, which would effect children attitude & mentally.

First we take *example of a family* with drunkard parents, whose one son became mayor of town. In a interview, he said that he knew from childhood that drinking ruins the family and decided to keep away from it and he worked hard for welfare and developments of his own and others in society at large.

But other brother, who had become a gangster, replied that he became same as he had his parents.

Both the explanation are right in their own way, it depends how children perceive and react to events happening round them. Even in movie, stories also have generally one or two massages or themes around which the whole story revolves.

Attitude of a person is very important, one friend showed one clipping in Newspaper that drinking is injurious to health and his friend responded that he was discontinuing from the same day. The friend was surprised how easily an alcoholic can leave drinking. Then the person explained that he was only discontinuing the Newspaper from the same day and not drinking.

We have *another example* of adding few germs into two jars, one containing water and second containing alcohol. Pointing to a drunkard to see germs in alcohol get killed but germs in water were healthy, drunkard understood that this means alcohol will kill germs in stomach, you can never beat their logic.

Let us take another example of *Hotel Room Boy*, who carries luggage to room and wait for Tips this regular type. Other Special type is that he cuts open the ribbon (Airlines wrap around) on the latch / lock of your baggage so their you can easily open your bag. He also checks the tea kettle working, tunes T.V, explains the channels and also guides you to set WIFI on your mobile phone. Though it may take him some time but saves you of many hassles, this what is called smart worker approach.

Negative People —WE HAVE NEVER DONE IT THIS WAY.

While working anywhere, You can always see Resistance & High Headedness of some of the pampered staff:

One such case - In our steel rolling mill, one 400 KW DC motor Bearing of roll-stand drive failed, causing mill to be down. Cost of mill downtime can be few lakhs Rupees per eight hour shift. We needed a Bearing with C-3 higher clearance, 4 inches bore big Spherical roller-bearing for repairing the motor. But it was not in our store stock and was also not in ready stock with Local bearing dealers.

We were informed by our purchase that two reconditioned bearings were available in Mumbai.

Being head of Engineering, I gave clearance for procurement of these bearings and next early morning, on entering the plant, found that bearings had arrived.

It's clearances was checked and I decided to use it, although clearance was little more than specification. Only one was required and gave instruction to fit it.

After morning tea time, during my plant round wanted to check progress of bearing fitting, but I was informed that bearings have been returned to the Vendor on the same vehicle. It was to my surprise.

On making enquiry, I found that my assistant & head of electrical Section, who came to plant later on after me, had refused to allow a reconditioned bearing to be fitted on electric motor in section under him. It was his statement that He had never used any such type of Reconditioned bearing on motor in his life and so got the bearings returned.

As urgent action was required, Management used its influence and resources & managed to get two new bearings. As I was very angry on disobedience in the department, This time, I kept away from the Bearing fitting activity. The bearing was fitted by maintenance staff under guidance of all the mechanical staff & Electrical Head and rolling mill was started by evening time.

On reaching home that evening, I got call from electrical manager Incharge that newly fitted bearing was running hot and already crossed 60*C. I advised him to stop mill immediately (as the bearing will get damaged due overheating,) and to cool it for half an hour and restart after re-greasing.

As I had to go for dinner outside, on return, I checked up with the section and came to know that bearing had failed after giving smoke, as the motor was kept working because operation Incharge did not allow to stop the Mill.

Next morning, our Director operations was already waiting in the plant office when we reached plant at 9 am. Obviously he was very angry and wanted an explanation. He found me equally upset when I asked him about what had he done to curb indiscipline in the dept. to bypass my instruction. As the electrical head was his favourite person he did not precipitate the situation and became soft and requested me to start the mill at the earliest, as the company was heavily losing due to non-dispatch of urgent deliveries. I assured him that mill be start without any further hiccups. Second bearing was fitted with precautions and mill was started by evening. This is called confidence in self and confidence of management in you.

Now, I will describe the theory and technology behind the events. Let us first understand mechanism of reconditioned bearings and not confuse it to the spurious bearings, which will be explained little later.

Big expensive bearings repair & reconditioning is a standard practice, where the bearings are dismantled and bearing track of inner and outer Races is inspected. If minor scoring is noticed then these are ground & buffed & same are used with New balls/rollers of correct dimension, material and hardness are inserted with new cage. To get desired clearance C3 or C4, different set of rollers are used. Reconditioned bearing received in the plant which I had permitted was done, after checking all the dimensions, including the internal clearance. It was not an adhoc decision. Though bearing internal clearances were little higher compared data in catalogue, but these were useable, under the situation. I had taken a calculated risk, which we need to do many time to keep the plant operative.

Now, let us examine failure of newly fitted bearing first time. Bearing fitting of new bearing was done with utmost precaution, particularly because of heated tense atmosphere, as I had boycotted & did not get associated with this activity. After fitting new bearing, which had internal clearances within limit as per catalogue, the team of all competent persons went to canteen to take lunch. To save time, they assigned juniors to put the end cover of motor, in which outer race of the bearing is slide fitted. On their return bearing was greased and Motor fixed on drive, after alignment.

After starting the mill, bearing temperature kept increasing. This can happen in many cases because of races of bearing may not be square in the housing and reduced internal clearances, due to higher interference in fitting. Many time, the bearing gets set by itself, after running for some time, but it needs a process of cooling the bearing by stopping it for half an hour and then starting. Otherwise the bearing will fail due to further reduction of internal clearances because of expansion of shaft and rolling elements, due to increase in temperature. As this process could not be followed by the electrical manager, bearing had failed.

Next day, the second new bearing was fitted by the same team under my guidance. I asked to measure all the dimensions again for this bearing also to understand what went wrong first time. We found that motor end cover bore was slightly oval which caused biting of outer race to further reduce internal clearance, much less than specified clearance. The bearing cover bore was scrapped so that it will easily slide fit on the outer race. In earlier case, we found that staff had forced fitted the cover.

This time also the bearing temperature increased slightly after starting, but mill was stopped for half an hour when temp crossed 60c, bearing was regreased and mill restarted. Bearing temperature stayed normal and normal operation started. Topic was never discussed again.

Case Study of other company:
In journal Bearings, grease grooves are provided in bronze shells. While going on shop floor round, I found that the mechanic/technician was fitting the bearing shells, without chamfering the grooves. I questioned him that grease will get scraped and will not lubricate the journal shaft, if grooves are not properly chamfered, to which he replied that he knows that. He pointed out that machining vendor is supposed to do this job, why should he (Mechanic) do extra work, when someone else is being paid for this.

I explained to him that vendor will do job as per drawing provided to him. Drawing in this case may not be showing this feature or even if it given in drawing, the, work-order may be only for simple boring of the bearing shells. And also, the engineer doing incoming material inspection may not know the importance of chamfering the grooves, so this never comes to light that the bearings are being fitted without chamfering, resulting in premature failure of bearings.

Maintenance personnel complain that bearings material is defective.

Oil rings:

Such is the case of bearings being lubricated by oil rings, as these get polished on its inside over a period reducing friction between oil-ring, so Oil ring moves Slow or does not rotate at all over the shaft, resulting in poor or no lubrication of bearings, causing premature failure.

– *Moral of Lesson* –

Equipment maintenance is a skilled job and correct procedure with understanding must be followed, otherwise unexplained premature failure would continue happening with blame games.

Chapter 28

"Installing Manufacturing Facilities with Minimal Investment"

In developed countries, there are companies in west making were manufacturing specialized products, consumed all over, since long time. When they go for modernisation and set up new efficient plants with higher Automation, they need to remove the old obsolete equipment of the shutdown plant to utilize space & the infrastructure for their future expansion.

In many cases, there are no takers of such Setup and mostly, they have to dispose it off as scrap, may be in some cases spending money for its disposal it.

Now, there are many Global broker Agencies who are active in making profit by selling it to small industrial houses in developing & Gulf countries, where labour is cheap.

Even some of Major Indian companies buy Industrial plots in countryside, where Tax Concessions are available, at minimum cost. They bring total facility and install here to operate the plant with local cheap labour. Market demand is already there, they only have to produce as per the specification.

If you can find an investor, then you to along with your associates can benefit from this route to build an empire for yourself. What is involved is buying of near scrap value plant, its transportation, cleaning, oiling & testing, erection & commissioning of the plant at tax incentive cheapest location for ready market, which is can be done is collaboration with the parent company of the plant.

Chapter 29

"Impact of Quality of Life on Quality of Product & Services"

Let us take case of a water pond, in which temperature increases over a period to above (say 60*C), the temperature at which creatures cannot survive, so the frogs inside get blisters and die one by one.

But any frog coming from onside will immediately jump out of Pond and save its life.

The point being highlighted is that the general population gets conditioned to environment in which it lives. For making any change, reaching Tipping point (Sufficient Population) Action is required, where adequate number / percentage is converted for the change to sustain.

Let us take an example of five monkeys in a Room with Banana Bunch hanging above the ladder, every time one monkey goes up to take Banana, balance monkeys are subjected to electric shock with remote controls, so they prevent any Monkey to go up the ladder.

After Some time, this system is de-energized but monkey family ensures that no monkey goes up the ladder. After some time, part of monkeys are replaced by new ones but still no one permitted by the group to go up over a period, even when all the Monkey are new but no one goes up and no one knows why but This is also the foundation of Customs and traditions in any place.

Way back, post operation infection was major cause of deaths in Indian Hospitals. Though we had good foreign trained Doctors and also one Doctors working in Prestigious Hospitals abroad used to visit to perform Successful open heart surgery, but there used to be frequent cases of patients not surviving. One of the factor was inadequate sterilization and sanitation standard in which patent was kept post operation. Then came awareness leading to the revolution of matching class Medical Facilities in Hospitals here providing sanitation and sterilization of international standard, Today, India has become Medical Treatment destination with cheapest packages.

Same in the with industrial Product Quality. While world class Management tools & techniques are provided to get six-sigma defect free product, the mind set of operating staff is equally important. As mostly the manufacturing work force has Rural back ground, where they are used in stay under sub-human conditions, They take time to develop sensitivity to Quality standards, precautions, safe-guards and use of necessary appliances.

For example, while replacing the Machine bearings or say, carbon- cup of Pump Mechanical seal, operator may not be sensitive to take adequate care and this itself can cause initial installation damage. As it takes time to reach a particular level in education, similar time & effort is required to achieve workmen skill to achieve product / Services of world class quality standard. So it is important that staff is sensitive to the gravity of challenges to be able to provide Quality Product, defect-free with timely delivery.

Employees' Family also need to have good quality life style, so that earning members can focus on their work.

Many brands have stood test of Time like Dhabur, Godrej & Tata's, while many other brands have failed.

Chapter 30

"Givers and Takers – in Business Dealings"

All the people in Business are there to make Money Quickly and as much as possible. Various people have their own method and approach to it. You go to a shop and ask for a Remote of T.V for example, shop keeper starts looking in its drawer, although he already knows that is not there so does not find and tells you that his boy who kept it has gone for Tea, asks you to you comeback after sometime and he would keep it ready for you.

You being a good customer, do not go to other shop and return to him. In the mean time he gets it from other shop.

In other case, you find that he really did not have that item but kept you waiting so that during the time spent in his shop, your might find some other item of you interest to buy. Shop keepers with poor sales want customers to spend time in their shop with the hope to sell something to them or to attract others passer by.

There are other shop keepers, where your take four Medicines but the fifth one in not with them, they quietly send their boy to get it quickly from next Medical shop and give you full supply. Some time the Medicine is not ready self item, they will get it later from their supplier and send it to your house, free home delivery. Some time you searching for some difficult item, the shopkeeper may guide you to where you will get it and you would be thankful to him and build up relationship with him. Generally shopkeeper's standard reply is that they do not know, although they may know where that item is available in nearby shop and you too develop a indifferent attitude towards them.

Then, there are many Takers, who interested only in their commission by making a sale deal. They may hide facts and encourage you to make bad deal like buying a Flat on the Bank of stinking Nalla or hostile Neighbourhood, as long as they can make money. In long run they may lose many good customers and their reference friends.

Our group was going for a big project and we approached our known source to do it for us but the Agency felt that this assignment could be best done by another company. They guided us to have best term for deal, sacrificing their chance to earn profit. Later on when another equally big requirement came, we placed order on this Agency. This way even by giving away their own interest first time, they got a lifelong dedicated client. In their way, by giving away an order, they got a permanent customer. This is called getting business by being a Giver.

Example of a boat painter's story will give us insight of quality work. One rich business living on lake side had an old boat, which he decided to repair and use it. He gave it for painting as he wanted to first get it painted. While boat was being painted, he suddenly had to go out of station and on his return, he did not find the boat anchored on lake bank, on enquiry he found that his family had taken boat for sight seeing.

He knew that boat had a hole in its bottom, making sure as it would sink with water entering into the boat, as it was lying unused for long time.

Visualizing that boat had sunk with families, he fainted, but on regaining he senses, he found that boat had come back safe with family safe.

He went to painter to give additional twenty thousand Rupees, besides ten thousand which he had to pay for boat painting. But the painter just responded, that doing minor repairs like plugging a hole was their way of providing Excellent Quality work to their customers. That painter was a Giver and as a result had built huge dedicated lifelong cliental.

Let us see an example of obedient worker, Boss asked his assistant to take out his car from the parking, as he was in a hurry. At we first red light signal, some one pointed that car tyres did not have enough pressure and he also noted that fuel gauge was showing empty. As he was in hurry, he had to park car on road side and he took Taxi to timely reach for, his scheduled meeting. So obedient worker is not goos enough.

The same Boss, while driving up will in a Ghat was told by his co- passenger, who was his Assistant that temperature gauge was showing needle in red, which Boss himself had not noticed. On checking they found only steam and no water in Radiator, after cooling the engine they filled water in Radiator. as hose was leaking and had to make up water few times, till leaky pipe was repaired. The car engine was saved by timely action which was possible by the observation of alert & smart co-passenger.

Chapter 31

"Think & Grow Rich – Make Money- involve Family Members"

Everyone wants to have more comfortable life and spend their life time to achieve it and only few make break-though. People get a job and grow in the organization or make change of job and finally retire with or mostly with or without pension.

For people without pension, most of them have to live on earnings from Interest, dividends or rentals of property, so the post retirement life becomes a challenge as the regular income discontinues and routine life expenses not only continue, even these keep mounting with time.

In most of the families, the next generation takes over in joint families or the old couple has to depend our their lifetime savings.

But few professionals go for second inning and use their core competence and official contacts to establish a business, where even the unemployed family member get involved.

Few examples will help to explain the concept. Some RTO people have opened Driving schools and also RTO Franchise Services, where the whole family is fully engaged.

Other, we see in Doctors or Dentist clinic which provides employment and also family members can be engaged. Catering and Tiffin services. Many Defence personal operate security services successfully, here too family member get opportunely.

So, we find that even a small businesses can provide full family with earning opportunities. But then, sometime it requires investment which a retired person is reluctant to risk his servings, but in case a younger member wants to venture, Parents can provide support.

Only very few business are making profit in short time but most have to go through few of the rough times and after a period only few business make good going but many have to close down also.

You will yourselves would see many new shops closing after some time and then other person with other product/services tries his luck. If business is operated on past experience or core strength, chances of success are higher.

There are few ideas for new business but you yourselves have to evaluate how practical and workable there are.

Have you ever thought of someone providing, five star candle dinner at home package, where smartly dressed persons as per your preference, bring in packed dinner, lay down dinning area & table and serve you five course dinner, then clean your dirty dishes and leave clean house. This type service can be for birthdays and other get together. Then total house cleaning, removing things, cleaning, then placing them back.

Chapter 32

Do It Right First Time and Every Time

Repetitive actives are many times monotonous and boring. When you perceive danger, you become alert and take all safety measures, known to you. If you stay in this situation for long, over a period, your senses begin relaxing and your alertness level starts going down. That is the time when accidents can happen. All the safety guidelines consider this factor, even working at height is unsafe and requires taking safety measures.

Normally standard scaffoldings are used for construction work. But for short duration work, ladders are used because a person can remain alert for a short period say half an hour but later on his responses start slowing and chances of falling increases. Basic points is all the safety guidelines should be strictly followed, otherwise we are inviting accident to happen.

No shortcuts otherwise they cut your short. For shop floor, Safety drills are also done so that concerned persons are kept in readiness for any emergency situations. These drill should be taken seriously, whether these are for fire fighting or to prevent unsafe conditions.

For example, when you enter a house and find gas leakage smell, you should not switch on electric fan, because a spark of electric switch can cause explosion as gas may be present in the rooms.

You have first open windows and doors to spell out entrapped gas,

For *doing things right first time and every time*, rigorous training, to develop understanding of the process, is required which makes the *operator subconsciously competent.*

For this he has to upgrade himself *through four stages*
1. first from being subconsciously-incompetent (, that means he does not know the danger of the process), ignorant stage.
2. The he goes to *consciously incompetent* (meaning he knows his shortcoming) and start learning the system.
3. This helps him to go to next stage of *consciously – competent* (like learning driving a car) and
4. well over a period, he get so used to its operation automatically that he can gossip or listen to music, as he does not here to pay particular attention, while changing gears or braking for his normal driving. This stage is called *unconsciously-competent.*

For operators to be safe & dependable, it is necessary for all the concerned staff to upgrade themselves to this *stage of unconsciously-competence.*

Multitasking is adopted for achieving higher Productivity in Manufacturing. For doing this, it is important that operators stay Focussed on their Job. Any Distraction can be risky. So, Multitasking is another factor for something wrong to happen, you need to focus on the main activity, you are performing to do it well. If you find it boring, you will not able to provide quality product or service. Take example of a mother packing

Tiffin for her child or doing dish washing, it is her love for the family which is the driving force. So everything she does is defect free good quality.

Your attitude towards your work also matters. We all knows about mother attitude and nurse attitude. With mother attitude nothing can go wrong but we also hear of baby falling from nurse's hand but never from mother.

Instead you read news that in case of accidents, where mother got injured but baby in her lap was found unhurt.

Yet another is safety discipline, you are taking risk and not following the safe method or procedure, you can escape most of the time but one time you can become a victim. Many accidents are result of such carelessness. It is what the analysis shows, when you take short-cut to save time and effort.

Example are many say crossing railway track under a standing train, which can start moving any time, or even crossing fast track traffic road instead using over head bridge or under ground path.

Ignorance of danger, we used to read in newspaper that one- time a lady got electrocuted while putting wet clothes for drying on live -electrical cable stretching though their compound, people or cattle also got electrocuted while leaning or touching the steel wire-rope provided to balance the electric poles. Reason was the insulator provided on the top had got damaged, so the leakage current passed though the it

While stacking tall fragile breakable tall items, care need to be taken that it does not fall down, even if it topples by accident, there should be a stopper, so safety mind set is very important. All the bolts and screws tend to get loosened over a period of usage due to minor vibrations, so periodic retightening is required.

Take example of kitchen pans without handle now, because their handle fell off due to its coming out of loosened screws. Take a look of your bathroom toilet seat which goes out of its position due to slackening of bolts, so retightening of bolts & screws is important activity, particular for equipment subjected to even slight vibration,

Quality of work on fixing safety devices again plays important role. You may have read of a battle lost because of a missing nail on horse-shoe. one king after having almost winning the battle with enemy army running away, fell down from his horse because horse shoe coming off, with soldiers thinking that their king was killed. The Enemy army came back and captured the kingdom. On investigation later on, it was found that black-smith was short of nails and while fitting the nails of horse- shoes did not fit one nail, due to which house shoe came out causing horse to topple for king to fall down.

Again, importance of quantity of work and product, Root cause Analysis of Ram's Banwas (Exile) was due to two wishes by king, Dashrath to queen kaikai, who had supported chariot wheel during a battle, if the quality of chariot axle had good, Ram would not have been sent in Exile and there would be no Ramayan.

– *Moral* –

Rigorous training and right Mind-set with practice can ensure Right First time & every time.

They rightly say Achievers don't do different things but Do Things Differently.

Chapter 33

Quality, Management & Growth – to Building Empire from No-where

A Very good example of Quality & Growth through sound supportive management of one company is described here. This company started as small Enterprise doing precision machining for making jigs & Tools. Customer satisfaction and good Business Development marketing put them with good order position.

To meet customer demand, they had to increase their machining & manufacturing capacity continuously to keep coping up with the increasing demand.

Procurement of more precision machines and setting up many more Manufacturing Units at various locations, depending upon the availability plots & ready sheds became a way of life for few years.

Company started with small machining activity but over a period, it diversified in various sectors to supply its products for export market. The Company always has good order bookings.

Company did have many challenges on the shop floor in various areas but these were being addressed in phased manner, as priority was first to increase machining capacity of the plants. Initially, frequent machine damage / accidents were happening, due to the operators not trained on that particular type of machine, Company was taking fresh operators to fill new vacancies being created with additional machines being installed in the plant.

There was need for an experienced machine instructor to check operators ability by taking their practical test and also training them with new operating features of machines of different makes.

Manifold increase in capacity and product diversity led to many challenges like requirement of higher skill operators to handle state of Art of Complex equipment including Robotics.

Machine layout changes required frequent shifting of Machines, Erection and commissioning all by in-house workforce. This required fast upgrading of skill of existing staff and selection of Competent new entrants.

Management system and infrastructure was modern and robust, management was very supportive for maintaining positive environment for employee's empowerment. Company Motto was *Leading with innovation*. Clear vision, Mission and five year action plan, all these were place and accordingly company had been achieving milestones of progress and capacity increase.

All the ingredients of a world class progressive company were being provided.

There was strong monitoring system with incentives and penalties according to group and individual performance. This was done by regular KPI – key parameters indicators performance measurement, based on percentage achievement level.

Integrated management system (IMS) consisting of ISO 9001, ISO 14001, & ISO 45000 were all operative with Risk mitigation and Continual improvement with kaizen gallery display of implementation of good ideas.

Employees Skill matrix evaluation was done periodically and section wise and level wise average was displayed on noticeboard for further improvements.

Word class advanced technology was being adopted for consistent quality and higher manufacturing industry, but company had its own challenges on manpower productivity for prime quality, quantity and safety. Company needed to employ high percentage of work force of semi skilled contract workers. They are generally utilised for material handling and support activities for regular employees. Their performance also effects the company outputs. Many companies take good care of their skill development of contract employees by providing them also opportunities to train them to do their job efficiently and safely.

Most of the company Manufacturing Plant Units operate independently and therefore the skill levels was different and also the standard of maintenance performance level.

For improving Productivity, Company had few years earlier engaged a reputed. Agency for upgrading their shop-floor working by implementing 5-S workplace organization system and implementing partial Autonomous Maintenance and even kaizen activities in older units.

As stated earlier, the company had taken massive expansion by adding many new units and part of manpower was sent to these new units.

Initially, focus being on capacity increase, so the confirming to standard operating procedures (SOP), working systems established by the expert agency, were compromised and that level of upkeep could not sustained. By this time, company has already achieved reasonable increased capacity and new units added also are of higher standard with latest machines.

These new units were also of high standard. Company has now already started to hire Technical Consultants to improve shop floor working system by adopting *Lean management* to achieve world class maintenance and TPM (total productive maintenance) with fresh full fledged autonomous maintenance.

Company has also set up separate training Department under HRD for Employees skill up gradation with university level course outlines for employees to achieve higher competence level.

By this time company had already achieved reasonable increased capacity and new units added also were of higher standard with latest Technology machines. Infrastructure of these new units is also high standard.

Company has now already taken initiative to improve shop floor working system by adopting Lean management, journey to World Class Maintenance and TPM Total productive maintenance with fresh full fledged Autonomous Maintenance.

Company has also separate training department under HRD for employees skill upgradation with university level courses available online for Employees to achieve higher competence level

Company output products are mostly being exported to western countries. On request of few Customers, company is selling up its manufacturing units in these countries, including USA, itself to meet faster deliveries and to save material handling. This is also providing the company employees with opportunities to grow up within the organisation to achieve their lifetime ambitions.

Expanding manufacturing capacity is a challenge but many companies in past have done it very well mainly by using their shareholders' money. But long term sustaining and maintaining growth was one area, where many failed in long run, as it required a different management strategy and approach.

In steel sector, many name like Ispat & Essar, Llyods, Uttam, ISMT, Bhusan had their ups & downs. In this case described above, management was ensuring a solid base for long lasting stability of operations.

Chapter 34

"Trusted Partnership Can Achieve Great Success."

Mostly people are hesitant to enter into partnership relationship because it is likely to break at some stage.

But many have proved it wrong. We will discuss two cases here.

One of them goes like this.

Few High level Professional employees of one company got together and set up one plant and struggled together and succeeded in stabilising the operations and one success followed one after one and they built up an Empire of group of companies.

Good example of synergy of committed group of people.

Another one is one chemical company is Ankleshwar and Dahej in Gujrat which we will discussion now.

Few friends there too got gather and started managing operation of one less making family owned company which was unable to sustain its working.

Now group up grated the technology and brought now technology and establish its name as supplier of Quality products.

With professional approach company could make good standing with customers and also increased its production capacity.

As product demand could not be net with existing unit, company went for massive expansion and become a big company.

Bigger size of operation with bigger manpower also brought many operation. Management did not appoint new outside Executive at senior positions but gave opportunity to old loyal employees through who management had successfully revived the old plant. All have been given higher responsibility and needed guidance to develop themselves to remain effective.

Management appointed technical consultant expert to gap study of their working practices so that manpower can effectively maintain and operate modern equipment effectively and safely.

Shop floor fee as many challenges one of them is trained complaint staff. Most of the employees are from the surrounding area which is not very developed technology and information data is well guarded by all the companies. So most of employees are evaluated by the compliance performance and obedient

There is not adequate systematic training of new staff & workers. Supervisors pond time on data logging and making reports other than work on equipment or supervision and checking technicians work.

Investigation of failures and reconditioning of Assemblies are mechanically done without in-depth understanding. Life & performance of repaired equipment is also varying from few months to over a year, because there is now disciplined methodology to get the assembly / equipment repair done within specified tolerances, with genuine spare parts, inspite of ISO 9001:2015 being in place, activities are mostly done mechanically.

There is a need of effectiveness audit in all the plants whether compliance is being done properly as per specified procedures. Normally, it is fill in the blank approach instead of improving system, and over a period it get diluted and deterioration is well visible while making Gemba walk (shop floor inspection).

Establishing a new working method requires all round effort throughout the organisation giving recognition to one convenor – management- Representative. Later on, sustaining it requires more effort as no one gets credit for it.

Deterioration over a period is always visible in all sphere of activities. Solution to this challenge is establishing a very effective kaizen & suggestion Box schemes with good implementation and follow up with rewards & appreciation system.

These chemical Industries clusters generally in isolated coasted Areas are prospering, very well except for few challenges like the employees become koopmanduk (Frog n the well), because of their very limited exposure to Industrial developments happening in business world, as the obedient Employees keep working like ox of the mustard mill, where ox with its eyes covered from both sides keeps going round a circle all the time.

Industry management system also sometimes encourages obedient Employees over smart workers resulting in lower performance levels.

Chapter 35

Pro & Con's of Big Manufacturing Plants – Located in Big Town / City

State Government gives permission to Companies set up their big / heavy manufacturing facility Plants away from Town / City. These Plants are generally located at a distance of 25 to 50 Kilometers depending on availability of big area plot. Their Staff staying in Town have to start by 7.00 AM and return home after 7.00 PM. As most of day time is spent far away from home, they can spend time with family only on weekly off day.

For Plants located inside the Town, Employees can meet their Family members outside the Gate even at Lunch Break or even take Gate-Pass to do Banking or other small tasks.

While recruiting new Employees, Choice is between Experienced Competent persons coming from other States and local ones with no specific Expertise or relevant experience.

Hence, company selects key position personnel based on the Expertise even if the person is from distant native place. These Employees are dedicated and go to their home town once a year, where as local staff goes on weekends and also take frequent holidays to attend functions in their family. So Productivity and loyalty of outsiders is higher.

Let me share about yet another mini steel plant of repute. Plant is located in a Metro City, providing luxury to its officers to go home even at lunch time or do their banking jobs. This is great attractions for employees in their job as it helps for family and children education.

Mostly manufacturing plants of larger size are normally located out of towns at longer distance of say 30 to 60 kms., Hence Employees have to spend even up to three hours or more time only for travel, beside their duty hours. In this way, these people spend most of day's time outside their home away from families.

Now we are talking of this company, where they have easy recruitment; people always ready to join even of at lower salary.

Although Plant equipment is old and not in great shape & working systems are also of not of high standard. Shop floor staff has to work hard to meet production and quality target but employees continue doing it without any complaints. Skill up gradation and supervisory development programme are not very systematically followed. In fact manpower is very lean & tight, plant managers are unable to spare their staff for training or other improvement initiatives.

Mangers in this company feel proud to spend longer time working in plant attending to routine repetitive problems and breakdowns and at the end of day informing top management that they are making great contribution in smooth operation of the plant depending on who is the sectional or Departmental head.

Improvement initiatives for energy saving and cost control can not given adequate priority as the staff is loaded with routine jobs.

There is brighter side also. Top Management lead by renowned Technocrats very well understand the situation. At one stage, they take up massive improvement programme by adding most modern processes and replacement plan. This changes the scene all together and Plant becomes a Model one. May be due to bigger operations at group level, such actions some time get done in phased manner.

Chapter 36

"Paradise Post-Retirement – Second Inning"

Energetic enthusiastic & young senior executive retire at the age of around 60 years as per company policies. But these people have the capacity for many more years to continue making value added contribution which is very well understood & accepted by the top management.

Many companies have schemes to derive benefit by employing them for second inning on contract basis at CTC (cost to company) at about two third of their last salary when they were position of authority. Assignments given to them may in advisory or supportive role to build up supplementing in company's new set ups. They can guide young Qualified but inexperienced Executives in Management responsible for factory operations. Smaller companies and ones not too strong financially have to pick up from the students or staff who could not make it to top list but once they join, they find them into a very learning & coaching environment which helps them to establish themself faster in the new organisation.

Blue chip companies takes cream of talents in campus placement and their other job offers.

This model is working very well for many groups which have number of limits or companies, where retired persons are given in location or plants other then wherefrom, they retired.

These retired officers are employed on three- or five-years contract and remain very loyal to company. They are keen to make their best contribution for the growth of the company, to remain in demand for renewal of their next contract.

– *Lesson* –

There are different school of thoughts. Most of company consider their Employees as communities and use them for their useful active life and then retire them.

But Few Company take their Employees as their family members and permit them to work to earn to maintain their living standard. Few even give them raise in designations by creating suitable position like V.P.s, Sr. V.P., Executive Sr. V.P. Presidents, Presidents and Sr. Presidents.

To mention few, Sir Inder Singh's Steel & Wire company in Jamshedpur – ISWP. was one and one in Khopoli, Maharashtra also. There may be many more.

Chapter 37

"Developing Top Management In-House"

There are different models in different companies to fill up their top management position.

In most of the companies today senior most competent person is picked up in house for take charge of the operations or else one is brought from in from outside.

Many reputed companies have the scheme of systematically preparing them to take fresh young persons as graduate trainees or Management Trainees. These Management Trainees are given all round training in different departments to learn working system and also provided practical fields & class Room training.

Few families run companies even go on to train the next chairmen on their shop floor to learn and understand operations and system like other to Company trainees. Their helps incumbent to understand decision making at top level. They are later on given independent charge of different departments to based on their capability.

They can have formal or informal procedure to select these Understudies. One in to pick up the best talent through their performance record, Interviews & Group Discussions and other can be informal where, Boss makes his pick and may also give chance to bright children's of their top Company officials.

In this process, top management able to groom incumbent to understand their thoughts and their policies are smoothly implemented throughout the organisation.

– Lesson –

Companies need to prepare a succession plan and train up the rights candidates to take up top Management positions.

It has been seen that the companies had to be sold off after founder Members retired, as there was no competent person with foresight could be developed to take the company forward, as these started making loss again, which was happening when their companies when these were just set up and started operations.

Chapter 38

"Rags to Riches – High Flyer Executive – Burning Candle Both Side"

While preparing for entrance examinations of professional Institutes or *IIT*'s, studying long hours past midnight is not uncommon to students, who have gone through it. That too with shoestring budget, who can afford only half stomach food due to paucity of funds available. This affects their health and also many end up having powered spectacles.

Even during the studies in professional institutes, situation is not much different. All want good placement and few lucky grab lucrative highly paid jobs and overnight their life style changes. They can now afford good food, high living, club membership and many other perks. But the competition of fittest continues, They accept difficult challenges and continue working long hours.

Even during the graduate Trainees in Reputed Company, they have to report in Training institute in other area at 6.00 A.M. for Physical Exercise, followed by two hours of class room session, then visit to factory up to 3 P.M. and again evening classes from 6 P.M. TO 8 P.M. Thereafter they can go for entertainment in club or elsewhere, and then do homework or writing works visit Diary upto midnight. They also have to be ready & prepared for surprise periodical quizzes, as failing in three quizzes their job & training gets terminated. Of course after failing in two quizzes, they get a red letter warning.

Most of the trainees get settled in regular departmental job, looking after their assigned responsibilities, then Tension level goes down and their life get a healthy routine.

But few high flyers with ambitions make effort into get in Management eyes by accepting difficult challenges and continue working long hours, attending late night parties and also doing extra-curricular activities, thus continuing to keep their Body and mind in overloaded mode all the time.

Human Body has capacity to stand overload condition for short period, beyond that it starts to give alarm failure signals. To maintain and grow in their status, these high flyer executives ignore these alarm signals and do not give their body any rest or relaxation. They may also attend Gymnastics or outdoors games with the hope of getting them relief.

But then, in high competitive Corporate world, We have seen many young senior executive & CEO's getting Heart attacks at early age of forties and dying on the spot.

Heart surgery or stents or pacemakers are not uncommon. This is part of professional hazards being in top management positions.

Beside this many of ambitious high flyers have been seen going for very early morning walk may be around 4.00 A.M., just because one of top bosses does that and to stay visible to him even in early hours of the day. This too taxes their Body to remain active for extra hours every day.

Besides all these engagements, Hectic travel schedules take their own toll on the health of these executives. They have to take early morning flight, by getting up at 2 A.M or 3 A.M., to attend meetings in other towns and return by late night flights back home and to be in office next morning at scheduled time. Sometimes they take overnight journey also for attending full day meetings next day.

This has effect on their families too, wife has to take care of household matters and children. Old ailing parents may also need attention, who may be staying in other location. Attendants are sometime arranged to look after them. But this gives added tension on the mind of these executives. Sometime they have to rush their parents to hospitals for urgent attention & Treatment.

– *Lesson* –

We people have seen these young CEO's for their lucrative packages but they are also paying a cost for it in terms of their health and family issues.

Chapter 39

"Journey of Transforming Plant Maintenance System to Upgrade to World Class Level"

Let us now see a journey of transforming Plant Maintenance System to upgrade it to World Class Level by implementation of robust maintenance methods.

We can start with study of how the maintenance activities being carried out, like Details of preventive Maintenance - PM Check sheets and how these are being carried out. This may include handling, storage & management of failed parts. Analysis of Breakdowns, why & Root Cause analysis, Kaizens done by them. Equipment upkeep and it's condition.

- All their PM Forms & formats are reviewed to make them more effective. PM check sheets Format is be revised and being covered in three parts,
  1. Inspection & CLT (Cleaning, Lubrication & Re-tightening) = AM (Autonomous Maintenance),
  2. Replacement of Components & Repair.
  3. Overhaul & Reconditioning Calendar.
- Skill Matrix format is reviewed for skill evaluation of all Maintenance staff, as was felt necessary and also to accommodate Company required Format.

- Lighting on Shop-floor: Translucent Perspex Sheets may provided in Shed Roof for day Lighting to get adequate light. Some time, Action need to be taken for suitable roof cleaning method so that Roof lighting becomes more effective.
- Further, Machines are generally dirty on its rear side, along with leaky oil. Rear side of machines is found to be dark. Arrangement for Inspection lighting should be checked, so that the defects on rear can draw attention. These points will be followed with concerned persons.
- For limited Shelf-life items and content in Containers with expiry date, specific monitoring needs to be fixed. It is mandatory requirement of ISO 9001: 2015. Accordingly, a documented procedure for its storage is under preparation, which should incorporated in ISO Manual after necessary approvals.
- *Centralized & decentralized Maintenance*:
  - Centralized Maintenance Facility & Monitoring: Idea of a Technical Cell & Central Repair Facility are examined. This ensures standard uniform working of all units for Coordination and Audits to improve maintenance effectiveness.
  - While this subject is being debated, All need to understand about the requirements of various CBM Instruments available for Monitoring Equipment Condition…for taking suitable Action. List of all CBM Equipment like Vibration analyzer which has been prepared to monitor Machine health as well as which need to be procured.

- *Areas for making improvement should be selected using the following criteria:*
  a) Those which have a positive impact on the work environment, for example Housekeeping.
  b) Relatively simple but with a tangible payback.
  c) If possible, choose projects in which the advice of members of the workforce can be of value.
  d) Make sure that the projects selected can predictably be completed and the results implemented in around three months from the beginning or less. People will loose interest if the projects go on for too long.
  e) Be very careful not to take on anything too challenging in the early days. A failure at this stage would be a major upset in the implementation process.
  f) Projects selected should be either measurable or countable
- Review of Pro-Active improvements in different Areas & Projects selected by various Work Units, using the following criteria, can being done.
  a) Those which have a positive impact on the work environment, for example Housekeeping.
  b) Relatively simple but with a tangible payback.
  c) If possible, choose projects in which the advice of members of the workforce can be of value.
  d) Projects Make sure that the projects selected can predictably be completed and the results implemented in around three months from the beginning or less. People will loose interest if the projects go on for too long.
  e) Be very careful not to take on anything too challenging in the early days. A failure at this stage would be a major upset in the implementation process.
  f) selected should be either measurable or countable

- SOPs (Standard Operating Procedures) for important repetitive jobs have to be prepared by various Work Units. There can be few jobs which are common to other Units. There is need for Review of these SOPs by Central Monitoring.
- Subject Matter Experts for Technical Support: List of Topics for Training to develop Subject Matter Experts for Technical Guidance and assist in all Plant Maintenance and Productivity related activities can be prepared,
- Corrective Action & Preventive Action - CAPA Reports can be made more effective, if CAPA reports include Root Cause, Correction, Corrective Action & Preventive action done.
- HIRA- Hazard Identification & Risk Assessment with Severity Ranking with Action for Significant Level need to be prepared.
- Even Safe Working Load - SWL of EOT cranes should be visible from Shop-floor by Boldly marking and also with Serial numbers Boldly marked
- Even Marking column Number, Bay Number are practiced by many Organizations.
- Maintenance Site offices can be mini Maintenance Knowledge Centre with most of the Units have their Trends Charts, Pareto Charts and also Cause & Effect Diagrams, which has given them for them monitor their performance themselves.
- Skill Matrix Evaluation with separate Parameters on which Engineers, Technicians and Managers was being evaluated as per Ultra standard for various levels. But need to be completed early.

- Review of Pro-Active improvements in different Areas & Projects selected by the Units using the following criteria is being done.

  g) Those which have a positive impact on the work environment, for example Housekeeping.

  h) Relatively simple but with a tangible payback.

  i) If possible, choose projects in which the advice of members of the workforce can be of value.

  j) Make sure that the projects selected can predictably be completed and the results implemented in around three months from the beginning or less. People will loose interest if the projects go on for too long.

  k) Be very careful not to take on anything too challenging in the early days. A failure at this stage would be a major upset in the implementation process.

  l) Projects selected should be either measurable or countable

- *For Computer Maintenance Management System- CMMS implementation and development of the CMMS database should be developed.*

Few more Initiatives as given below can be Taken:

- Increasing Effectiveness of Maintenance work by increasing amount of Planned Work
- Implement sustainable processes for Maintenance operations with best practices
- Ensure the sustainability of the installations by making action plan for increasing the life span of the Equipment.
- Promote "best in class" productivity levers (PMR *(Preventive Maintenance Routine);* criticality; spare-parts; prioritization; active supervisions; etc.)

- Document and share best practices and continuous improvement initiatives
- Organize and structure the completion of FMEAs on critical systems
- Set up a critical parts inventory strategy and update it regularly
- Measure and analyze maintenance KPIs in order to support the next strategy orientations or improvements to be planned.

A. *make Preventive Maintenance more effective.*

For this, information of total man hours used in the month for Planned Jobs & unplanned Jobs. Pareto Chart displaying Vital few contributing maximum Down Time can be Displayed in Maintenance Site Office. Root Cause study to done to take action to Tackle major factors.

B. Another List of Chronic Problems under various categories 1. Problems which can be resolved by Section itself. 2. Problems for which Expert Advise and Outside or Senior Management Support Required.

C. Inventory Optimization: Store can requested to provide information on Non Moving Items. Spares, Slow Moving Spares.

D. Following areas also need to be examined:
  - During PM tasks – how Inspection and lubrication of existing equipment being done
  - CBM tasks – Condition based monitoring of faults and failures using appropriate techniques
  - Management of Spare parts & inventory
  - Use of Visual displays for increasing awareness.
  - Motivate Staff to implement Improvements to get Benefit of Kaizens

Chapter 40

"Safety First in Industry – Best Dividend"

Accident free safe working is viral for smooth uninterrupted operation of any plant, while installing any Equipment or designing manufacturing process, even at Design stage, consideration to all safety factors must be given.

Japanese say that *Accident do not happen, they are caused.* Therefore it is necessary to identity the cause of hazard and to eliminate it or provide means to avoid it.

Mostly at work place, Importance of safety- guards is not seriously taken, and sometime after repair work, the machines are started without putting back the safety- guards. New Employees or semiskilled workers are also unable to see the Danger and become victims, more often.

Even the old qualified officers also miss out the Hazards points. En example given here will give better understanding, A technician working on pit side of Steel Melting Shop crane at 18 meters height had fallen down, while a doing routine inspection and preventive maintenance job and immediately died. His sectional head in charge went up to investigate the cause and he too fell down and died. Later on the helper described the situation that head- gap between the two Crane Girders was small, where the technician was doing his job and after completing his work when he got up, his head hit the top girder causing him to lose his mental balance and he fell 18 meters down on the hot steel slag and same thing repeated for supervisor, who went to investigate. It was quite unfortunate.

Preventive measures required would include formulating SOP (standard operating procedures) for taking adequate safety measures to prevent such occurrences while working at Height. A whole set of Safety system for *work at height is now mandatory* for Employees' safety. This includes medical Fitness Test of Employees working at height. Employees need to have all safety protection appliances and full body Harness with adequate life line system and its training for persons, while working at height.

While working on shop floor many short cuts are taken which cut short the protection and cause accidents. Another example of fatal accident is of Ajit Singh a crank staff gridding lathe machine operator. He had taken a simple job to machine a portion of long steel rod of three inches diameter. The rod had a overhang on the rear side of the lathe with no centre support. On starting of lathe machine, the rear position of rod bend increased with speed and caused severe vibration of the lake machine.

Electric Main switch of the lathe on the other side of rod, the lathe operator rushed to switch off electric Power and was instantly hit by the bent edge on his head, as he could see the rod flying & rotating at high speed. He was killed on the spot, quite an unfortunate accident.

There is no end to list of such avoidable accidents which could have been prevented, if Hazard identification study was undertaken at work place and training was undertaken.

Safety Department is considered to be the Agency responsible to prevent Accidents. In fact it the top management which is most responsible for its approach towards handling and implementing safety principles. Many Managements are in *Compliance mode* that all the regulatory guideline are followed. Few management take safety seriously, from Design stage itself and ensure no unsafe condition or working practises are allowed to be present in the work place.

Chapter 41

"Charting Our Course Forward"

In navigating the winds of the corporate world, we've explored the impact that everything from training programmes to business partnerships can have in shaping an organization's culture and performance. While each company's journey is unique, some universal insights have emerged:

> The power of leadership - especially in times of crisis and change - cannot be overstated. Executives who lead by example, communicate transparently, and balance short-term execution with long-term investments can steer their organizations through stormy seas.

However, toxic and unethical leadership also has consequences that permeate throughout an organization's culture.

Mind set shifts are challenging but not impossible to cultivate. With a combination of incentives, training, and leadership messaging, organizations can gradually improve on its attitudes and behaviours. This not only applies to employees but also to shifting customer and stakeholder perceptions.

Agility and innovation are competitive advantages, especially for smaller players but bureaucracies move slowly. Smaller, nimbler competitors can outmanoeuvre them through rapid decision making, flat structures and constantly evaluating new opportunities. However, achieving it also has benefits - resources, stability, branding and Finding the right balance is key.

Partnerships, when aligned around shared values and complementary strengths, can achieve exponentially more than the individual players alone. However, partnerships can also fail without mutual trust and transparency. Joint ventures around the world have illustrated both the synergies and pitfalls of partnership models.

Perhaps most importantly, we've seen there are always multiple paths to achieve a goal. Conventional wisdom isn't the only factor. Disrupters appear and reset industry standards. A solutions-first, employee-focused, high integrity approach to business can ultimately be more sustainable and profitable than a short-term profit maximization approach. But old habits die hard.

This examination was not meant to be exhaustive, but I hope it has provided thought starter and illuminated some timeless realities of human nature - our strengths, our flaws - that remain consistent across eras.

As the corporate landscape continues to evolve, how do we chart the right course forward, without losing our way? Here are some parting principles, I find helpful:

Stay continually curious and keep exploring new vantage points. The day we stop learning is the day, we stop growing. Remember business is ultimately about people, not just numbers. Foster human relationships and trust.

Measure "success" through the lens of integrity and purpose, not just profits. Stay grounded in ethics and values. And finally, have the courage to think differently, speak candidly, listen deeply, and contribute meaningfully. We all have roles to play.

I am optimistic about the future and our ability to chart a course forward that benefits not just shareholders, but employees, customers, communities, and our world. Calm seas or rough, the journey continues. Let us voyage on together.

Message from *Rear Admiral D V Taneja (Rtd.),* *Ex-Chairman- MD, Indian Seamless Steel &* *Alloys Ltd., Pune.*

My Comments on Book on *Navigating through Corporate World -Some Challenges -Impact of Company Culture on Performance & Results* by Harcharan Singh.

It is my pleasure to introduce Mr. Harcharan Singh, Author of this book, who has more than 50 years of experience in plant engineering

and operations roles. In my interactions with me from the time I have known him as a very soft spoken, humble technocrat

who used to believe in teamwork and help all his subordinates to grow to their potential by giving the required legroom, guidance, and encouragement.

One of his specialties was that he always shouldered responsibility and held himself accountable for the function

that he was heading and acted as a perfect shield for his subordinates to perform and blossom under his able leadership.

He was also a perfect listener and receptive to suggestions and ideas from cross-functional teams.

And above all, he never lost a chance to express his frank opinion.

His book is about corporate culture and performance. As an organization evolves, its culture and capabilities evolve

with it. Some of the key factors that impact corporate culture, sharing stories of companies who succeeded in transforming themselves

- and those who failed. From small, family-run businesses to giant conglomerates, certain principles apply across the board.

He has touched few key questions: How do you influence positive change in mind-sets and behaviours across an organization?

Companies live and die by their culture. We'll look at the impact of training programs, work rituals, incentives structures and leadership.
What does it take to turn an underperforming asset into a high-performing one. How can companies generate more value from what they already have?.

How do some small companies build empires, while others stagnate.

Mr Harcharan Singh has shared his experiences and thoughts in the form of this book and realized his much-cherished dream of his authoring his own book.

I am sure, the industry fraternity and Corporate world would be benefitted by his practical sharing of his thoughts and experiences.

My best wishes to all the readers with the hope to see most of you achieving great milestones by learning and practicing lessons give in this book.

Wishing him all the best

Regards

Rear Admiral DV Taneja, VSM, IN (RETD)

Ex- Chairman/ Managing Director

Indian Seamless Steels and Alloys Ltd., Pune

Comment's of *Mr. Vinod Garg, Ex- Executive Director -Ispat Industries on Book- Navigating through Corporate World - Some Challenges & Impact of Company Culture on Performance & Results & the Author- Harcharan Singh.*

It is my privilege to introduce Shri Harcharan Singh.

I can vividly picturize him in my interactions with me from the time I have known him as a very soft spoken, humble technocrat who used to believe in teamwork and help all his subordinates to grow to their potential by giving the required legroom, guidance, and encouragement.

Happy for Mr. Harcharan Singh that he has finally penned his experiences and thoughts in the form of this book and realized his much-cherished dream of his authoring his own book. I am sure, the industry fraternity and Corporate world would be benefitted by his practical sharing of his thoughts and experiences.

Wishing him all the best

Regards

Vinod Garg

Ex Executive Director-Ispat Industries Ltd

(now JSW Steels Ltd)

and currently Chairman of Vibrant Global Group

JINDAL SAW LTD.

Dear Reader,

It is my privilege to introduce Mr. Harcharan Singh, Author of this book, <u>Navigating through Corporate World – Some Challenges</u>". A versatile technocrat who believes in teamwork and help all Shop-floor staff to grow to their potential by giving them guidance and encouragement.

There are several qualities of the author which you will see while reading this book. The first one is versatility and completeness. I looked at the contents and it practically covers all aspects of a Corporate experience. One cannot come up with all these points unless one has been sufficiently grounded in the way Corporate functions.
He is a Senior Technical Consultant, Mentor, and Industrial Trainer for Plant Productivity Improvement & Skill Upgradation. Mr. Harcharan Singh has now shared his experiences and thoughts in the form of this book and realized his much-cherished dream of his authoring his own book. I am sure, the Industry fraternity and Corporate world would be benefitted by his practical sharing of his thoughts and experiences.

Wishing him all the best

Regards,
Dinesh Sinha

08/02/2022

President
Jindal Saw Ltd.,

A-59-60, Malegaon MIDC, Sinnar - 422113, Distt. Nashik, Maharashtra Phone: +91 (2551) 227200 Fax: +91 (2551) 230967
Corporate Office : Jindal Centre, 12 Bhikaiji Cama Place, New Delhi- 110066 • Phone: +91 (11) 26188360 - 74, 26188345 Fax: +91 (11) 26170691
Regd. Office : A-1, UPSIDC, Indl. Area, Nandgaon Road, Kosi Kalan, Distt. Mathura (U.P.) - 281403 • Website: www.jindalsaw.com
CIN: L27104UP1984PLC023979

Message from Dr. PNN Iyer, is an Economist.

"**H**archaran Singh has been among the top trainers, coaches & mentors in the field of Excellence in Manufacturing. A meritorious Master Metallurgist with a post graduation in Management from XLRI, his career spans over four decades with world class, large, listed Corporates.

Widely travelled as a consultant, trainer and mentor, his passion for exacting standards, proven procedures, innovations, productive culture & down-to-earth practical methods make him a sound source of learning, implementing, monitoring, adapting & creativity in the shop floor, design studio and the R & D Labs. Quality management at the macro & micro level has been his Forte at a global level.

All those who have the humility to keep learning will find this book very valuable."

Dr. PNN Iyer, is an Economist specialized in Globalisation. Widely experienced in the MNCs & TNCs, rose to being the MD; was instrumental in 34 international collaborations.

Message from Mr. Venkatram Bala Subramanian
- Ex- CEO- Kalyani Carpenter Special Steels Ltd., Pune -

Shri Harcharan Singh is a doyen in the field of engineering and Management with decades of practice. He has brought out the nuances of management both engineering and Management, blending his practical experience and expertise with aspects of manuals based on theory.

I know him personally for more than two decades and was witness to many of his contributions. The treatise is a document to be preserved and practised by future generations which should benefit individuals, corporates besides Contributing to national growth

Another significant aspect of Mr. Harcharan Singh's presence in the corporate world is the Passion displayed in every activity undertaken by him. I wish every one of us imbibes this great quality which will a fitting tribute to this young old gentleman.

Mr. Venkatram Bala Subramanian
Ex- CEO- Kalyani Carpenter Special Steels Ltd., Pune

Author the Author

Harcharan Singh.

B.Sc. (Mech) Engg, MBA [XLRI], F I E (IEI [I]).

Ex-Asst. DM -Tata Steel Works, Jsr., Ex-Head of Engg. & GM (Tech) ISMT, Pune & Ex-Head of Engg. Ispat Industries (now, JSW), Nagpur.

Principal Technical Consultant, Coach, Mentor and Industrial Trainer.

Plant Productivity Improvement & Skill Upgradation

Mr. Harcharan Singh is B.Sc. (Mech). Engg. with Post Graduate Diploma in Mechanical, Electrical & Steel Metallurgy and MBA from XLRI, Jamshedpur, has specialised in plant engineering and maintenance activities. He retired, as Head of Engineering & GM (Tech), from ISMT ltd., Pune. Earlier he worked as GM (Engg) for 5 years in Nippon Denro Ispat, Nagpur (now, JSW Industries) & as Asstt. HOD for over two decades in Tata Steel plant, Jamshedpur.

He Senior Technical Consultant, Mentor and Industrial Trainer for Plant Productivity Improvement & Skill Upgradation. With rare combination of experience in varied areas & successful implementation of Quantum modification & improvements in different plants, he is now offering his Consultancy and training in Plant maintenance Engineering for World class standard, Productivity improvement for Employees' Skill up gradation and Quality Management Systems.

He has conducted over thousand seminars, workshops & Training Courses on Various Technical & Shop-floor Productivity Improvement and Management Topics.

He has also executed Overseas assignments and attended Seminar workshop. He conducted Training Workshop in Nigeria. He has been Technical Consultant for many Reputed Manufacturing Companies.